MISS

Charlie Hedges is one of the UK's foremost experts on missing persons, particularly children and those who are abducted and trafficked. During a career spanning thirty-six years, he worked in the police force, eventually specialising in missing persons in 1997. Charlie has amassed a wealth of experience with the UK's leading public bodies for missing persons, joining the UK Missing Persons Bureau in 2008, then the Child Exploitation and Online Protection centre in 2012. He has been involved in some of the most high-profile cases of recent years and was awarded an MBE for his tireless efforts in the protection of endangered missing children by Queen Elizabeth II in 2015. *Missing* is his first book.

MISSING

My life finding the lost and delivering justice for the living

Charlie Hedges

SEVEN DIALS

First published in Great Britain in 2024 by Seven Dials,
an imprint of The Orion Publishing Group Ltd
Carmelite House, 50 Victoria Embankment
London EC4Y 0DZ

An Hachette UK Company

1 3 5 7 9 10 8 6 4 2

A CIP catalogue record for this book is
available from the British Library.

ISBN (Paperback) 978 1 3996 1618 8
ISBN (eBook) 978 1 3996 1619 5
ISBN (Audio) 978 1 3996 1620 1

Typeset by BORN Group
Printed and bound in Great Britain by Clays Ltd, Elcograf S.p.A.

MIX
Paper from
responsible sources
FSC® C104740

www.orionbooks.co.uk

I have called you Rob in this book to give you some anonymity, but you deserve a special place here because you changed my life, for the better. You gave me a new purpose to improve things for those who go missing and their families. I hope my work has been beneficial and diminished the myth of 'just another misper'.

CONTENTS

GLOSSARY OF KEY TERMS

ACPO – Association of Chief Police Officers
CEOP – Child Exploitation and Online Protection
CSE – Child Sexual Exploitation
ICMEC – International Centre for Missing & Exploited Children
Misper – Police term for 'missing person'
MPB – Missing Persons Bureau, now the Missing Persons Unit (MPU)
MPIH – Missing Persons Information Hub
NCMEC – US National Center for Missing and Exploited Children
NCOF – National Crime and Operations Faculty
NCPE – National Centre for Policing Excellence
NPIA – National Policing Improvement Agency
PEN-MP – Police Expert Network on Missing Persons
PolSA – Police Search Advisor
PRAS – Police Research Award Scheme
SAR – Search and Rescue
SOCA – Serious Organised Crime Agency
TVP – Thames Valley Police

PROLOGUE

Every year in the UK, there are on average 350,000 missing incidents reported to the police.

One every ninety seconds.

Why a person has gone missing is unclear when they are first reported, but that is where the case begins.

Who are they and what's going on in their life? When were they last seen and how did they seem? Is there anything that makes them particularly vulnerable? Does their age, a mental or physical health condition, or something else put them at risk? What sort of environment are they in? Have they had any problems recently, or are there any relationship issues that might have led to this point?

I look at the time of day they went missing and consider the weather and terrain and ask myself more vital questions.

What are the immediate and obvious reasons for their disappearance?

Have they chosen to go missing?

Has a third party been involved?

As a picture begins to unfold, it's my job to work out the best way to find the missing. Often, the hairs might stand up on the back of my neck as I anticipate a challenging case, or a shiver runs down my spine as I spot something that could lead us to the missing person. Or, I fear the worst, and my heart sinks as I think of the impact on the missing's family and friends.

This isn't going to end well is an all-too-familiar phrase that lodges itself in my head as the investigation continues.

In difficult terrain or poor weather conditions, I fear that they may have come to harm as a result of an accident, and mobilise search teams to scour the area. Where there's evidence of mental distress, I worry that they may harm themselves and hope that we find them in time. Where there's an indication of a serious crime my concerns increase, and we explore ways to not only return the person, but also to end the criminal exploitation.

I anxiously review how long the person has been missing. Are we still in the 'golden hour', when witness memories are fresh, and vital evidence is more likely to be found; or has that opportunity been missed and we're on the back foot?

Either way, speed is of the essence. I begin to join the dots, developing a number of hypotheses which change, are added to, or deleted, as information and evidence grows.

This person – any person – deserves the best response possible from investigators, but that response must be appropriate and proportionate. Do we need a search plan, media appeal or criminal investigation?

Searching for the missing is never a tick-list exercise. No two cases are ever the same, even if there are similarities. The right action must be taken at the correct time; there's no sense throwing resources at something just to check a box and be seen to be doing something.

As the hours tick by, you hope beyond hope for a swift resolution, constantly reviewing and reassessing the information and investigation approach as the situation shifts with every passing minute. Looking from every angle, considering every opportunity, and trying to solve the puzzle.

Someone is missing. How do we find them?

INTRODUCTION

Keep Calm and Carry On

I did not intend to forge a career around missing persons. If you had told me that I'd end up travelling the world to discuss the topic and be instrumental in developing national and even international policies and frameworks, I'd probably have told you that you were mad. The more I have thought about this, the more I have realised that my upbringing and experiences in life were instrumental in enabling me to achieve what I have.

I was born in Reading, Berkshire in 1953. My mum and dad already had three girls, my older sisters; Annette or 'AJ' being the eldest, Maureen or 'Mimi' in the middle, and Susan or 'Sue' who, despite being the youngest girl, was still thirteen years older than me.

Throughout her life, Mum would tell anyone who wished to listen that when she found out she was pregnant with me after such a long gap, she would go to church and cry because she didn't want to go through it all again. This anecdote never made me feel insecure though, as I never had any reason to doubt the love of either of my parents. Our family unit was tight; how lucky was I?

Following the tradition of altering names, I morphed from Charles to Charlie, as my given name seemed a little formal. Mum and Dad were older parents to me, but they were very happy to have added a boy to their brood. The large age gap between my sisters and me meant that they were already adults by the time my earliest memories started to develop. When I was four years old, AJ went to live in Australia, and Mimi followed a year later. With a long sea voyage, only letters for communication, no mobile phones and certainly no video calls, the move was a much bigger step back then than it is now. With both sisters moving away and Sue being thirteen years older, I grew up very much as an only child. I didn't want for love nor company, but I did learn to be comfortable on my own. I could entertain myself alone for hours on end and use my initiative to complete tasks that I might have leant on my older siblings to help me with, had they been around, a skill that certainly became useful in later life.

My sisters had grown up through the war years, but I was fortunate enough to come shortly after rationing had ended. As the country emerged from the war, opportunities grew and my parents were able to enjoy the fruits of their hard work, something they instilled in me as essential if I wanted to succeed. My dad was self-employed for most of his life, running a range of businesses in Reading: a hotel during the war, then a butcher's then two fish and chip shops. Mum's working life began in childcare, before taking some time out to raise the family, eventually returning to the workplace to support Dad in his business of the moment. It was only much later in life that she had a job in her own right, firstly running a school canteen and then in a haberdashery shop, followed by the childrenswear department at Heelas – now John Lewis – in Reading. She adored children and I still remember how her eyes would light up with joy when surrounded by them.

While my father was very independent, he was also very aware of the social divide, as was the fashion at that time. Growing up I saw him as being quite deferential to 'important' people and those in senior positions, something that made me feel that elevation was not possible. In some ways, this inhibited my ambition until, as I matured, I learned otherwise. Later on in life, as my work saw me argue and negotiate with senior government officials, speak in the European Parliament, meet prime ministers and even Queen Elizabeth II, I came to understand that they were all just people.

My childhood took place in a time with many more freedoms and fewer concerns about safety, enabling me to roam freely and do things that parents of children today might never allow. Gaining my own sense of independence and being allowed to find my own way was always encouraged.

My grandparents on my dad's side lived in a village about two and a half miles away and, from a young age, I was allowed to cycle by myself to visit them. I'd fly down country lanes, taking deviations as suited my whim, enjoying the beauty and vastness of the countryside as I went. Nature was a big part of all our lives.

It wasn't just that things were safer back then, or that I was particularly fearless, but my confidence exploring the world outside came from the way my mum and grandmother talked about nature to me as a child. They always made me aware of its importance and how everything was connected to it. When Mum talked about the wind and sun, she spoke of how they felt, giving a real sense of their part in my world, and mine in theirs, so that I always felt comfortable and embraced the outdoors.

My parents actively encouraged my independence and I was allowed to walk the half-mile to my local primary school, Earley St. Peter's, on my own, as was the norm in those days. I was brought up to think that when faced with anything, getting the job done was the primary goal and giving up was not an option. This was mainly derived from Dad, as he was a very practical person, doing lots of jobs around the house and garden, finding solutions to problems and always completing the task, no matter how difficult it was.

One winter's morning, when I was about nine years old, I set off on my usual walk to school. Ice coated the ground, but trousers were not allowed, so I braved the chilly conditions in bare legs, wearing my regulation school shorts. I'd only travelled about fifty metres when I lost my footing and fell to the ground cutting a large wound in my knee. Turning round and returning home didn't even cross my mind. I just carried on. By the time I arrived at school, blood was running down my leg and squelching in my shoe. Even then, it wasn't me that alerted my teachers to my bloody leg, it was a girl in my class. Wound promptly cleaned and dressed, I remained in school for the rest of the day.

It was an early indication of what was to become core to my work ethic, and I still have the scar on my knee as a reminder today. Everything my parents instilled in me and everything they did was aimed to give me the best chance in life. After leaving Earley St. Peter's, my parents had me join a public school, the Reading Blue Coat School. As determined as I was, I quickly discovered that I was not really an academic. The strictures of school life and being cooped up in a classroom did not suit me, and I spent much of my time longing to be able to be outside, roaming free. Each year there would be an end of year service for those who were leaving – or as I saw it, escaping. I still remember my confusion at the first such service that I attended, when I witnessed a boy crying with sadness at leaving. It wasn't the crying that baffled me, it was that they were tears of *sadness*. I was already certain that any tears I would shed when my time to leave came would be those of joy as I escaped the monotony and routine of school life.

Over my years at school, I learned lots of things about life and relationships but did not fare well at exams, struggling to get five 'O' levels, even having to stay on an additional year to do that. I was far more interested in activities such as rowing, canoeing and cycling, the latter two being hobbies I shared with my best friend, Simon. We enjoyed many adventures together. At fourteen years of age, our slightly eccentric history teacher suggested that six of us go on a cycle tour for several days, starting from our school at Sonning on the Thames, passing through the Chiltern Hills and then continuing to Houghton Mill in Huntingdon, returning on another route through the Chilterns, staying in youth hostels along the way. On the day of departure, we were all geared up and ready to go, apart from our teacher, who was having problems with his old upright, 'sit up and beg' bicycle.

'You boys go ahead. I'll catch you at the first youth hostel,' he'd said.

Of course, we agreed. What freedom to be rolling through the hills, unsupervised, at that age! When we arrived at the hostel several hours later, our teacher was still nowhere to be found. It emerged that he'd set off, covered a short distance, then fallen off his bike, leaving it severely damaged and himself injured. Although not serious, the injury meant he would no longer be able to accompany us on the trip. Without teacher supervision, you'd expect that to be the end of our fun, but it was a different time then. We decided together that we had to get the job done and would continue alone, so we did. Following the planned route, it was just us, the road – and some concerned questioning at each of the youth hostels about how we were being supervised.

The independence that my parents had encouraged in me served me well, despite my lack of academic success. I had a weekend and holiday job from the age of fourteen, starting in a local grocery store, and when it came to leaving school, I set my mind on a career that would combine the hobbies that I enjoyed with earning a living. Our family holidays involved camping, hiking and educational things like visiting famous buildings and churches. The latter was not my favourite, but as we conquered Snowdon, Helvellyn, Cader Idris and many others, walking became a great love. It was not without the odd temper tantrum and complaint about the length or steepness of the chosen walk, but I soon began to understand that was the challenge you had to navigate to earn the exhilaration of reaching a peak, soaking in the views, and looking back at what you'd achieved.

When I left school at seventeen, I intended to train to be a surveyor for the Ordnance Survey, making maps. I knew I didn't want to be doing anything academic, or to be chained to a desk. I wanted my work to combine elements of being outdoors, undertaking practical tasks such as drawing and amending maps, so the OS seemed like a good opportunity. I was getting on with my training and enjoying my first venture away from home, when one night Mum and Dad rang the family that I was staying with and asked them to tell me that they were coming to visit me.

'We'll come down and we can go to a local pub,' was the message that was passed on by my landlady.

'OK, I'll see them later,' I said, puzzled.

It was an unusual occurrence for them to spring a surprise visit on me, especially as Romsey was more than an hour's drive from home, but I didn't think too much about it.

I noticed they seemed very sombre. We sat down with a drink and Dad looked at me.

'Charles, I'm afraid we have some bad news,' Dad said. 'Simon had an accident on his motorbike and is dead.'

I could barely comprehend what I was hearing, as my parents explained that Simon had been found on a country road next to his motorcycle.

My best friend? My companion in so many adventures? This couldn't be right.

I was the reckless one who got into scrapes. I was the one who had the more powerful motorbike and crashed it. He had a little Honda 50 and was always careful.

Simon had always been the one who tapped me on the shoulder and told me that it was not sensible to do whatever new thing that I had just dreamt up.

It was so unfair, and I was devastated.

The scene was investigated, but there was no explanation for what had happened. As I came to terms with his death, we were all left with so many questions. *Did he lose control of his vehicle? Was it an accident involving a third party who had left the scene?*

Our questions were left unanswered. All that we knew for certain was that Simon was gone. I was close to his parents, who had also taught me so much as I grew up, and his older brother, John. We bore the loss together and remained friends for many years. It was a heartbreaking time, but sharing our grief meant that it was easier to deal with, knowing that we were not alone. In our still relatively short lives, we had shared so much and were very close. His loss was a great sadness to me and one I carried as my life continued. But his death also taught me an extremely important lesson about pain and grief that followed me into my work, helping me to understand others receiving devastating news or experiencing loss.

It was hard to do, but I carried on, doing the best that I could. I felt that I was progressing well and was enjoying the job, but after a few months, I had a personal interview with my director.

'How do you think you're getting on?' he asked.

'I think everything is going fine,' I replied.

'I am sorry, but I don't agree,' he said. 'You don't have what we call an "eye for the ground". You cannot interpret what you see and transpose it on to the map.'

'Oh,' I replied, unsure of what else to say.

'Take the weekend to consider if you should perhaps resign,' he said.

As I figured out my next steps, I realised that I really had no idea what I wanted to do, beyond not wanting to be constrained by routine. When I shared this limited information with an advisor at the local career advice centre, I expected to be probed further. Instead, she looked at me and said: 'My dad was in the police and that seemed to be an interesting job.'

Interesting was good enough for me, and without too much thought, my new career was decided. My early life had unknowingly steered me towards the path I would take. Joining the police seemed like a good idea, but I never imagined just where it would take me or that it would be a turning point not just in my career, but in my whole life.

CHAPTER I

On the Beat

I applied to join Thames Valley Police as a police cadet, because at eighteen years old, I was not old enough to be a constable. My lack of consideration about my new career was immediately evident, as I found myself disappointed that I was not able to do a 'proper' policeman's job, investigating crimes, arresting people, and dealing with incidents, rather than just being an observer. My early days in the force involved me in community work that I found gave me a much greater understanding of other people's difficulties and disabilities, and how that might affect their behaviour or make them more vulnerable.

My first posting in the regular force was to Cowley, a sub-division of Oxford, and my first boss was an inspector named John McKeown. He was strict but fair, was always at the forefront of any difficult or dangerous incident, would never socialise with his team nor allow anyone to admonish them. That was for him to do, and he considered any failing to be his responsibility as leader.

He did not speak directly to new probationers for the first two or three months, until he thought they were 'OK'. His instructions came to us via the two sergeants, who took it in turn to be responsible for either the patrol staff or the paperwork. A third sergeant, the station sergeant, who was not part of our shift but worked alongside us, oversaw the running of the police station and custody suite.

It was a highly disciplined operation, covering twenty-four hours a day with four shifts, with one team being on a rest day while the other three worked. The skills I had developed in community work proved useful as a new constable. Being a visible presence and getting to know the local people helped to build trust and gave you contacts that you could call on.

The relationship between the police and public was different back then. There was greater compliance and more certainty of enforcement if you did find yourself on the wrong side of the law. There was also more respect for authority and greater trust too, which meant we were more deeply embedded in communities. On most of the foot beats we worked, there would be a pub and in most of those a pint of beer was left out by a private entrance to refresh the local police officer. We always knew of places to go for a cup of tea, especially on nights; the sewage pumping station, all-night factories and bakeries, to name a few. At one bakery I would make the tea for the bakers and was even given the job of putting the jam into doughnuts to help them out.

As we laughed and chatted, I discovered more about the people, their lives and their troubles, sometimes learning of things that helped in preventing or detecting crime. Even the criminals we dealt with were more respectful and gentlemanly! On one occasion, I stopped a suspicious vehicle on the Oxford ring road leading me to arrest the driver for fraudulent use of vehicle documents. He resisted and a short fight ensued before I put him in handcuffs.

We went to court a couple of days later. Outside the courtroom, he came up to me and shook me by the hand.

'Sorry about the scrap, Mr Hedges,' he said. 'I was doing my job to escape, same as you were doing yours, no hard feelings?'

'Not at all,' I replied. 'I won!'

My regular beat was the Blackbird Leys estate. It was a difficult area then, but nothing to its state today. In 2022 it was named the most dangerous small town in Oxfordshire, with 129 crimes per 1,000 people.[1] At twenty years old, walking those streets, I thought I was being the archetypal local beat bobby, befriending and helping the people in his neighbourhood.

I encountered a man who lived in the area and seemed to have lots of personal problems, so I decided to do my best to help him and visited him quite regularly. One day I popped by, only to be told that he had taken his own life. It emerged that he had been building a gun in a locked room to prepare for this act.

I was shocked not only by the news, but by the realisation that he had been doing this after I had l left him in my self-righteous state. The job certainly made you grow up fast and this incident made me realise how wrong you could be in your assessment, what could be going on behind closed doors, about the impact of your actions, and how easy it was to miss important signs. It was an early lesson in thoroughly questioning everything you were told or thought you knew. Some things could only be learned through experience, not in the classroom or from a book.

After a couple of years on foot beat, I decided that the traffic department was the next step for me. As a man in my twenties, patrolling large areas of Oxfordshire in fast cars and attending exciting and glamorous-sounding incidents appealed to my sense of adventure and dislike of routine.

---

1   www.crimerate.co.uk/oxfordshire/blackbird-leys

One selection process and an initial advanced driving course later I moved to a different office in the station and was allocated my first traffic patrol car – an ageing two-litre Ford Cortina. A second driving course followed, and I passed as a first-class advanced police driver.

Traffic officers worked in pairs, known as crew mates, one of whom was assigned to me as he joined the department. His name was Mike Rice, and we developed a special partnership. We knew how each other worked and thought and were often able to anticipate the other's actions in difficult situations.

We spurred each other on to work hard. Drink-driving was so prolific at the time that we would often go out at night and have a relay of arrests between us. When one was in custody with a prisoner, the other would go out and arrest another drink-driver and while that one was being dealt with, the other would go out and arrest one more and so on throughout the night.

Although we worked brilliantly together, we were quite competitive too. When there was the potential for a good arrest there was a race to be the first out of the car, unless the driver had 'accidentally' parked it close to an obstruction, keeping his partner inside, or the passenger found himself handcuffed to the seat. It was something that wouldn't be in line with health and safety today, but there was much less emphasis on such things at the time. It was just a little harmless fun to alleviate the stresses of a difficult job.

As well as healthy competition and great determination, the job often required us to find some 'outside the box' solutions. We had problems with a young prolific car thief who one night, at the age of 15, decided to steal a 52-seater coach. We located him and started to follow but it was too risky to try to overtake such a large vehicle and try to stop him. The pursuit, at a sedate speed of 40 mph, lasted for more than four hours, before a colleague persuaded a lorry driver to park across the road giving him nowhere to go. With no other option the teenager obliged by indicating left and pulling to the side of the road, where he was arrested.

It wasn't all fun though. In fact, being a traffic police officer could be extremely traumatic, especially when attending the aftermath of bad driving and traffic accidents. I remember one particularly brutal period of several months when Mike and I were dealing with a fatal accident every month.

One rainy night, working with a temporary crew mate, we were called to an accident involving two motorcycles, their drivers and one reported passenger in a very rural area on the perimeter of RAF Brize Norton. The scene was a dark country road with no road lighting and featured a bend on an incline over a bridge, with a T-junction in the middle of the bend.

Two motorcycles and three people were scattered across the road. We only had car headlights and some torches to provide light, but it was quickly apparent that two males were obviously dead and the third person, a girl, was in a very bad way.

She was clearly in pain, having breathing difficulties and had multiple injuries, the most obvious being that the sole of one foot was touching the back of her head. She needed immediate attention, so she had to be our priority.

Assistance was scarce, due to the usual weekend demand on resources, and being in such a remote area, there was a long wait for the nearest ambulance, and we were a long way away from anything else. Looking at the girl's condition, we knew the outlook wasn't good.

As we worked out what action we needed to take, a car suddenly appeared through the darkness and pulled up alongside us. A man emerged and told us he was an anaesthetist from the RAF base and had come out to assist.

By sheer coincidence and amazing good luck, he had been developing a device to solve issues with injured patients having breathing difficulties, identical to those the girl was suffering. We were able to leave him to look after her, still waiting for an ambulance as the rain fell steadily.

Clearly the bikes had collided head-on towards the middle of the bend and, judging by the scattered debris, the combined speed on impact had been considerable. There was simply not enough evidence for us to get all the answers to what had happened, something that had echoes of my childhood friend Simon's accident and death.

Eventually an ambulance attended and miraculously, due to the wonderful coincidence of the anaesthetist's skills and tools, the girl was expected to survive.

All that was left was to clear up the scene and make sure the road was safe for traffic. As I took a last look around the area, I looked over the bridge to a stream that passed under it and made a horrifying discovery. A fourth person was lying with his lower half in the stream, face down. I scrambled to the stream to help them, but on closer inspection, I realised that the casualty – a young male – was dead.

I was shocked and felt a sense of guilt. Had he drowned? We had arrived on the scene less than fifteen minutes after the accident happened. We had been there for three hours. If we had noticed him sooner, could we have saved him?

Had we failed to do everything we could?

The post-mortem showed that his death was due to the impact of being thrown from the motorcycle, not from drowning as I feared. It also transpired that the witnesses had been mistaken and both motorcycles had pillion passengers. Much later, I was fortunate enough to meet the young girl who was so horribly injured and saw that not only had she survived but she had made a good recovery.

There was no doubt that we saw and experienced many traumatic things, but I did not feel that I had much difficulty with the gory side of accidents – it was part of the job. I once attended a fatal road accident, put my hand into a bag just behind the driver's seat of a crashed car to try and find some identification, only to find that his brains had fallen in there in the impact of the accident. When the casualty was alive and conscious though, it could be a different matter.

I recall interviewing a man who had been a front seat passenger in a car when it had turned right in front of another car. He'd remained conscious throughout and told me in graphic detail how he felt the floor pan buckle under impact and the pressure increase on his thigh until he eventually felt it snap. Even my strong stomach lurched at the thought, described as vividly as it was.

Experiencing situations like these were part of policing and there was little time in the thick of an incident to do anything else, or it would not be possible to do the job.

Did it give me nightmares? No. Did those thoughts linger with me? Yes, sometimes, and not for any specific reason. But, at the time, the 'grin and bear it' mentality got me through; there wasn't really an alternative. I now know that wasn't necessarily a helpful approach, and as the years have passed, I have felt more emotion from recalling these incidents from my memory than I did at the time.

Although I didn't experience the difficult emotions there and then, in any situation like that accident, where something was missed or a mistake was made, I would always question myself as to whether I had done all I could.

I didn't and still don't see a way on from that, because to stop that critical reflection I would have to give up caring, something that I have never wanted – nor been able – to do.

CHAPTER 2

What's Next?

After several years in traffic, I was itching to move on. My new ambition was to become a dog handler, working with specially trained dogs to help detect and prevent crime, find lost or missing people, sniff out drugs and protect property.

As well as being varied, it required a significant degree of problem-solving, working with a trusted four-legged friend, outdoors in all weathers. Dog handlers were required to be on call regularly, responding to incidents any time of the day or night. Given that I did not enjoy regular nine to five work, that suited me just fine.

After three months' residential training at the force training centre at Sulhamstead, near Reading, I passed the dog handling course and was offered a place at Newport Pagnell. The busy and growing new town of Milton Keynes was on the patch, and I knew there would be plenty to keep me occupied, so I accepted.

Successful dog handling required a well-trained and capable dog with a handler who understands the dog and can interpret its actions. I worked with many dogs over the years and had successful partnerships, but my favourite was Dutch, a German Shepherd 'general purpose' dog.

Dogs trained in 'general purpose' would be used for crowd control, in security duties, to chase offenders, and search for people or property outdoors or in buildings, tracking by following any scent on the ground. This was distinct from more specialised 'mantrailing' or 'scent detection' dogs, who would be given an item with an individual's scent – a piece of clothing perhaps – and tasked with following that specific scent.

Dutch had a wild streak in him which meant that he was extremely effective, but it also meant that I could never really relax with him as he was always eager to hunt and chase.

Working one night shift, we received a call to an incident in Wolverton at about 2 a.m., where a colleague had stopped a car that they be believed to be stolen. The two youths in the vehicle had run off and back-up had been called to help track them down.

I responded immediately and was only given a vague description of the young men and the direction in which they had run. It wasn't much to work with, so I decided that the best tactic was to go on the hunt with Dutch. He would respond to any human scent in the area, indicating that someone was nearby, and would be able to follow it, hopefully leading to the offenders. This entailed going alone, not using a torch, and maintaining radio silence, while keeping Dutch on a rope lead. All these precautions were to minimise any noise or visual cues that might give away my presence.

By the light of an occasional street lamp, I guided Dutch around the streets following a search pattern and waited for him to indicate where the two men might be. Soon enough he started pulling towards a yard at the back of some shops, paying particular attention to a pile of wood. On closer inspection, we found one burrowed beneath the pile. He'd done a pretty good job of hiding from view and an officer alone would have missed him, but he couldn't outsmart Dutch.

I quietly arrested him and handed him over to a colleague, to take him back to the station. One down, Dutch and I set off to find the second person.

Before long he was once again pulling me towards another yard, this time behind a pub. As we reached the back of the building, I immediately sensed the presence of another person, so I flicked my torch on. The face of a young man was illuminated in front of me.

'Police,' I stated clearly. 'Stay where you are, you are under arrest.'

I moved towards the young man, expecting a straightforward arrest. But he had other plans. He started waving his arm around and I noticed something in his hand. Quickly I realised he was brandishing a Stanley knife.

'Go away or else,' he yelled, clearly aggravated.

It was dark, and, as was his wont, Dutch didn't bark, so it was likely he wasn't aware I had a dog. I decided to make the situation clear.

'I am a police officer with a dog, put the knife down,' I shouted firmly and as calmly as I could in the situation.

It was hard to remain completely calm when being threatened with a knife at close quarters, as I knew the failure to control the situation properly could have a painful outcome. I was, however, confident that Dutch would defend me.

'You're lying,' the young man growled. I repeated my warning, but his aggression continued to escalate, and I gently pulled back on Dutch's lead, knowing that this would be a signal to him. The man suddenly lunged forward, waving the knife at my face.

I let the rope slip through my fingers and Dutch shot forward. He rarely barked, almost as if he didn't want to give the game away, but he knew what he had to do. The expression of shock and pain on the young man's face was enough to tell me that Dutch had bitten him.

Police dogs were trained to make the difficult decision whether to bite someone who refused to stop, or not, if they were not running away. In these cases, they would just bark to scare the offender into stopping, also letting the handler know what was happening. But they seemed to know when biting was the only option. As Dutch sank his teeth in, the knife went flying and I made my move.

'I told you so!' I said, grabbing the man, before adding, 'You are under arrest on suspicion of stealing a car.'

The ability our dogs had to make that split-second decision always amazed me. The connection I'd had with animals when I was growing up meant I'd always had great respect for them. But their intelligence in this line of work astounded me. They could read things in situations that we couldn't, and their importance in policing shouldn't be underestimated.

At times, we had to put all our trust in their instinct, which wasn't always an easy decision. During one week of night shifts in Milton Keynes there had been a series of strange incidents on a small industrial estate, involving burglar alarm boxes and other property being damaged, sometimes by a shotgun being discharged.

There was no explanation for these incidents, but we formed the opinion that it was leading to something else happening. Sure enough, a few days later a call came in at 1 a.m. from a KFC takeaway on the same industrial estate.

The staff had been closing for the night when three men, armed with guns and knives, had forced them to hand over the night's takings and then run off.

I quickly arrived on the scene. The building was surrounded by tarmac and concrete surfaces, the hardest type of surface for a dog to locate scent on, but Dutch got to work.

Tracking requires the dog to locate and follow the most recent human scent at the point at which he is asked to commence his search; in this case, the back door of the restaurant. Dutch picked up a scent and off we went into a nearby housing estate, eventually reaching a point where there were several directions in which we could continue.

I was waiting patiently for his decision when Dutch suddenly dived into a nearby bush. Amidst an almighty commotion, I thought that Dutch might have found one of the offenders, but it turned out that something else had caught his attention — a rather feisty cat.

After the feline made its escape, Dutch emerged from the bush and immediately returned to the task at hand, casting around for the scent of our human offenders.

It had been an amusing incident, but at the time, it had me worried. *Had he overshot the location in his haste?* I wondered.

But I had to put my trust in him. I eased him back along the row of houses, until he decided to go through a gate into a garden. When he got to the door to the house, he sniffed the door handle and stopped. He did not want to go any further. This was where the scent had led him.

We didn't have armed response vehicles in those days, so I had to request that a special armed response team attend. This needed authorisation by a superintendent. It was always a big step, but on this occasion, it was even more important that we got it right. A couple of weeks earlier some incorrect information had led to armed officers forcing entry into a house occupied by innocent people. No one wanted a repeat incident.

Dutch and I maintained watch on the back of the house from the cover of some trees in case someone tried to leave. The request went up the chain of command and officers of ascending rank came to ask me if I was sure this was the house.

Each time I told them I was confident it was the correct house.

By this point, I should have been off duty. When my observation point was taken over by another officer, I returned to the control room, but I refused to leave until the case had been resolved. It took some time, but eventually a firearms team arrived, were briefed, and went to the house to force an entry.

The tension in the control room, where the operation was being managed, was palpable. As the firearms officers entered the house, we all waited nervously until a message came through on the radio.

'We have arrested three suspects,' the officer said.

The weapons and money from the robbery were also found hidden inside a rolled-up carpet – a successful outcome all round. I'd trusted Dutch's instincts and it had paid off.

My time at Newport Pagnell spanned seven years and there had rarely been a dull moment, but familiarity in the role meant it all felt quite routine, even if it wasn't a regular nine to five.

As I reached my fifteen years' service and realised I had only another fifteen before retirement, I began to feel reflective and to crave something that was more intellectually challenging. I had made several attempts at the promotion exam in my early years in the police, which would have elevated me to a position of supervising other officers and given me more responsibility, but I had never passed.

Try as I might, I couldn't see a way ahead in the police. I resigned and started a business in the world of sales, then learned that an ex-colleague, Paul Catlin, had started a driver training company called 'Drive and Survive', together with Ian Mason and Mike Rees, who were also ex-police. The business trained company car drivers, successfully reducing the number of accidents that they had. I started working for them as a trainer.

As well as having the opportunity to drive fast cars on the race circuit, alongside road training, I also started to travel abroad. I delivered training to drivers in Prague in the Czech Republic a year after the Velvet Revolution, as people were adapting to life after communism, had a brush with a gun-brandishing police officer in Hungary after being falsely accused of speeding, and endured a terrifying high-speed taxi ride to the airport in Poland. While perhaps not the intellectual stimulation I'd been seeking, it opened my eyes to many countries and cultures that I might not otherwise have encountered.

While I was always employed and generally happy at work, my career path was not a stellar one and I was experiencing relationship difficulties as well. It was my second marriage that produced one of the biggest and most important challenges of my life when, in January 1989, our son Tom was born. Earlier in my life I had not been that keen on the idea of having children, but Tom changed all that immediately. Having a new life to care for was amazing and a big responsibility.

I loved my dad, and my mum too, but the relationships when I was growing up had been much more at arm's length. It did not mean we loved each other less, it was just the way it was. When Tom came into my life, I was determined that it would be different. I wanted us to have a different kind of closeness, with the ability to talk openly to one another and have shared interests. Even though he was just a tiny baby, I was keen for him to learn about nature, as I had from my parents, and I hoped that he'd share my love of the outdoors.

As fun as 'Drive and Survive' was, I did not want to commit to years of driving the thousands of miles that this line of work entailed, especially not as a new parent. Being away for long periods of time wasn't the right thing to do; I wanted to be a hands-on dad.

In January 1992, I applied to rejoin the police – a secure and stable job – and was accepted, based on my previous good record, and was again posted to Milton Keynes, but this time to the sub-division of Bletchley.

On the surface, my transition back into policing appeared easy. As I crossed paths with old colleagues, many were amazed that I had been away for nearly five years. I slipped back into the camaraderie and community as if I'd never been away, but there had been dramatic changes in the law, such as the introduction of the Police and Criminal Evidence Act 1984 or 'PACE' as it was known. It was an Act that governed all the major police powers – investigation, arrest, detention, interrogation, entry and search of premises, personal search and the taking of samples, and fundamentally changed the way the police did business. Prior to PACE, for example, interviews with suspects were not recorded, but written up from memory later, and there had been less regulation concerning how long they could be kept in custody without charge. PACE dramatically changed processes and procedures, and how police conducted investigations, changing practices that had been used for many years.

Despite this attention to process and procedure, there was no formal one for rejoining. It was a case of 'Oh, you've done this before, just carry on.' My previous service in the police had taught me how to manage situations where a solution was not immediately obvious: slow things down and an answer would emerge. It was unnerving at times, but starting over gave me fresh determination. One of my main goals was to pass my promotion exam to sergeant and after two years of hard work, I succeeded. Shortly afterwards I was offered the position of sergeant in the force control room.

It was very different, and I wasn't sure about being confined to working indoors, but it presented a lot of new challenges, especially for a newly promoted supervisor. I was keen to rise to those challenges and give it a go.

Based on the top floor of Milton Keynes Police Station, looking out over the new city, I was responsible for managing the team, which received notifications of incidents occurring in the northern half of the Thames Valley area. My team was mixed, with civilian staff and police officers. Among the staff, a few had more than fifteen years of experience and knew everything there was to know, making them efficient and reliable. Others were a lot newer and less worldly-wise and needed more guidance.

The team was responsible for managing the radio and taking telephone calls. The calls were both non-urgent, often concerned members of the public reporting suspicious behaviour, minor crimes, and many missing persons, as well as 999 calls relating to major and critical incidents, such as homicides, public order, traffic accidents and crimes in action, which took precedence. It was our job to decide what the initial police response should be and deploy the appropriate resources.

Following a verbal handover from the supervisor going off duty, I would start each shift at the supervisor's podium, the force's computer system screens and my reference documents in front of me, and the wall-to-wall windows looking out over the town behind me.

From there I could monitor everything that was going on in the area, listening in on calls coming in to the radio and the telephone operators and speaking to my colleagues who were scattered around the control room, working in smaller teams.

Decision-making was a huge part of the role. When a call came in, there were always considerations. *How urgent was the need? Did we need to send someone straight away or could the response be slower? What resources were available and where were they?*

As well as dealing with the reports that were immediately in front of you, having an eye for anything that could potentially become an issue and giving it early attention was key too.

Sometimes it wasn't outside problems that needed addressing with urgency. There were internal things to manage too. Generally, the team came together well and fulfilled their duties to the very best of their abilities. Listening in on the radio I always tried to be mindful of personal stress issues and things that could be impacting individual members of the team, noting anyone who might need help or support.

But overhearing these conversations, on occasion also raised red flags within the team. There was one police officer I was just not happy with at all – I couldn't put my finger on it, but I was uneasy with his behaviour, so I started listening in on some of his calls.

I realised he was building a relationship with a woman who lived in one of the estates across the road from the station. I was shocked as the woman had come to us as a vulnerable person. The officer's behaviour was completely inappropriate; he was taking advantage of her.

Almost as soon as I noticed, the situation escalated, and I heard him arranging to meet her after work. It was all I needed to put a stop to it immediately, but not all issues were as easy to spot and, in some cases, went unnoticed until it was too late.

I worked on shift rotation with a fellow sergeant called Alan. He was a larger-than-life character, sometimes divisive and always ready with a story to tell. We would often have a laugh and a joke together and got on well in what I would call a 'robust' manner.

One night, as I came on shift, we had our usual, ordinary chit-chat and then he briefed me on what jobs were current and those that needed my special attention. Then he left to go home.

The shift came and went, and I returned the following night expecting to get his handover as usual. But he was not there.

'Where's Alan?' I'd asked.

'Haven't you heard?' the sergeant I was taking over from said. 'He was found dead this morning. Suicide.'

I was numb with shock. I'd only seen him a few hours earlier and he'd seemed fine. I knew from personal experience that life wasn't always what it appeared on the surface, but he was married, had kids, a good job. Everything appeared steady. Whenever I came across him, he was lively, opinionated and so full of life. What could possibly have happened to drive him to this?

I couldn't help but wonder what I'd missed.

Another occasion when hidden problems surfaced was when I was working on a problem-solving team. A colleague with a wife who was considerably younger than him did not turn up for his shift with no explanation. One of the team went round to his house but there was no answer, so a formal check of the property was arranged. To our horror, he was found hanging in the garage. His wife's body was later found buried under the patio.

In time, it emerged that he had killed her and then taken his own life. It was a truly shocking case, and we all had thoughts about what we could or should have done differently. But we didn't really talk about it. The general attitude was to learn from what had happened and move on.

In the force control room, I quickly gained a fascinating insight into the breadth of what happened across the area, learned to think on my feet, and developed a far better understanding of how sometimes even matters that seemed unconnected intersected.

It was extremely challenging and at times stressful, constantly having to juggle limited resources against competing demands. *Do we attend this job first? Is this one more important than that one?* I still longed to get back outside, working on the street in different places and meeting different people.

When I was invited to take a sergeant's post at Bletchley, with responsibility for the area beat officers, I decided to go for it.

I had no idea that shortly after, a note from my inspector would change the course of my career, and my life, forever.

CHAPTER 3

Case One

*Is the person vulnerable due to age,
infirmity or any other factor?*

It was never a note you wanted to see on your desk at the start of a shift. I was accustomed to coming in to a pile of papers, cases that needed my attention. But when one was top of the pile and accompanied by a handwritten note from your inspector, it was rarely good news.

'Can you sort this out please, Charlie?'

Well, I did always like a challenge. I picked up the three A4 sheets on this day in October 1997 and a handful of other documents that were bundled together and started to read them, approaching the task at hand methodically.

Top of the pile was a missing persons form. I heaved a sigh. Dealing with missing persons – or 'mispers' as they were known – was a regular feature in every police officer's life, but not always a task that was relished. In fact, it was often regarded as a nuisance, with the same young people going missing repeatedly, and hours of time spent on people who turned up of their own accord, or searching for those who didn't want to be found.

The information in the documentation was scant. I learned that a 19-year-old man named Rob had travelled by car from his home 200 miles away with a friend, to attend a rave at The Sanctuary in Milton Keynes. But he had never returned to the guest house they were booked to stay at.

When they came to leave the following day, his friend couldn't find him anywhere, and he hadn't returned home.

I knew the venue well, as all the officers in the area did. It was a warehouse on a small industrial estate that was opposite Mount Farm Lake, a former gravel pit that had been filled with water in the late 1920s and later developed into a green space for local people.

There was a grassy expanse of open space between the estate and the lake, leading down to a wooded area at one side of the lake, with knotted reed beds at the end closest to the industrial estate, all just a few minutes' walk away from The Sanctuary.

Ecstasy was the drug of choice for ravers, and illegal raves out in the sticks had been a thorn in the side of many police forces up and down the country throughout the nineties. There had even been a drive to create legal venues aimed at controlling the situation and making them safer, and The Sanctuary was one such venue.

But the drugs still got in, and we were constantly picking up the aftermath.

In fact, the problem had been exacerbated for several months as a particularly bad batch of the dance drug had arrived, we believed, from the Netherlands and was circulating. As well as people ending up hurt, unwell or in dangerous situations that we'd be called to attend to, the dodgy pills seemed to induce even higher levels of paranoia than usual. We'd be inundated with calls from young people in states of panic, saying that they imagined bad things were happening to them.

'*I'm being chased.*'

'They're out to get me.'

'They're going to take me away, I need help.'

It was a complete nightmare.

With the bare facts in front of me and what I knew of the venue and local area, my gut told me the outcome for Rob wasn't going to be a good one. In any investigation it was always important to develop a hypothesis or hypotheses, based on the available information and evidence at that time, to consider what might have happened, while always keeping an open mind to other possibilities.

The problem was, not much of an investigation had happened. As I leafed through the pages in front of me, it was abundantly clear that the way Rob's disappearance had been dealt with was poor, to say the least. It was a bloody mess.

For starters, no one wanted to take ownership of the case. The investigation had been batted back and forth between 2 force control rooms 200 miles away from one another, with each arguing that the responsibility to investigate lay with the other.

'He was last seen in Milton Keynes, so that's most likely where he's gone missing from. You need to open the investigation.'

'No, he lives in your region, he's missing from there. If you need anything doing, let us know.'

The stance of the police force from Rob's area was reasonable, but the back and forth meant vital time had been wasted. Responsibility had eventually landed with Milton Keynes midweek, following the weekend of Rob's disappearance.

Those officers who had been involved in the interim had done what had been asked of them, making enquiries at the guest house where Rob had been staying, trawling through command and control logs and dealing with local media who had got wind of the story, but it was all scattergun and reactive. There was no strategy to move the investigation forward.

The lack of ownership at the start of the case also meant there had been no structure in terms of keeping the family informed, causing a further strain when they were already deeply worried. Even worse, on reading comments from Rob's mother, Laura, I realised that no one had really been listening to her.

She'd acknowledged that he was a young lad, out to have fun, but she'd been adamant too that, 'We are close. If he wasn't coming home as arranged, he would have let me know.'

She had made it very clear that Rob's behaviour was out of character. This must have been indicative of something, yet there were no obvious factors then that made him 'vulnerable', in policing terms.

He wasn't a child or very elderly and there was no indication of a physical or mental health issue. Despite Laura's protests, the officers had clearly seen that Rob was a nineteen-year-old man and didn't consider him to be at risk.

Shaking my head, I exhaled slowly. Everything I'd read was a cause for concern. There were so many questions to be answered regarding Rob's movements, and there hadn't even been a real search of the area. We needed to up our game, and fast.

I set to work, looking at potential searches of the area near the venue and open area around the lake, and deploying officers to make enquiries after briefing them fully on the case. I liaised with police from Rob's hometown and researched other potential lines of enquiry.

I'd started my shift at 2 p.m. By 7 p.m. the two officers that I'd sent out to speak to leads that hadn't yet been followed up returned with important information. A local security guard had seen a person fitting Rob's description running around and acting strangely about 5.30 a.m. on the night of the rave, midway between The Sanctuary and the lake. They had examined the CCTV at the premises, and he could be seen outside the premises in the location described by the security guard.

Two people who had been in a van nearby had also reported a sighting. They'd described Rob in detail and explained that they'd felt he was vulnerable and disturbed, so they'd offered to help him. When they invited him to sit in their van, they described his behaviour as paranoid and said he'd run off saying, 'No, no, no, you're going to kidnap me.'

One of the officers I'd sent out was Rich Power. He was ex-military and very grounded. He and his colleague had used their initiative to find answers.

'Sarge, I think these sightings were our man,' he said. 'We have checked the area down to the side of the lake and could not find anything that might be relevant.'

We agreed that the timeline, the descriptions, the behaviour, everything fitted together.

Using all those factors, alongside Rob's attendance at an event at The Sanctuary where the use of ecstasy was common, I began to form my hypothesis. A common effect of taking the drug was the user feeling hot, leading to a desire for water. Rob's movements indicated he was near the lake – had he been trying to get down there?

I concluded that there was a strong possibility that he'd taken the drug, started overheating, gone into the lake . . .

And possibly drowned.

Searching the area to try to locate him or anything to show that he had been there was imperative and could prove or disprove my hypothesis, but as it was October, we'd already lost most of the light. I knew we'd struggle with the more complex search areas, but what if there was something obvious out there, a piece of clothing, a possession, even a body?

I trusted Rich and the other officer who had made the enquiries, but I wanted to be doubly sure that nothing had been missed, so I spoke to Rich again.

'How thorough was your search?' I asked. 'Given that there is a strong possibility that he went into the lake, is it possible there is something you missed?'

'We did look for anything obvious, but it was only a quick check,' he replied.

That was perfectly reasonable in the circumstances, but it meant we needed to check again, now. The last thing I wanted was to delay the search until morning, only to find something we'd have fallen across if we'd just walked around the night before.

I was not a trained search officer, but common sense and experience were telling me that given the length of time since any sighting of Rob, this was not a search and rescue situation, which implies saving life.

I was happy that it was not necessary to call out specialist search teams trained in seeking a live subject, but I decided that myself, Rich and the other officer needed to attend the scene and do another thorough search immediately. I also requested the police helicopter to make an aerial search of the lake shore.

As the lake was in an urban area, the glow from nearby street lights, homes and offices provided some light, but what we could see was still limited. We were doing the best we could in the circumstances, but care had to be taken that important evidence wasn't trampled or damaged. Footprints, fibres of clothing, even the smallest thing could be vital in piecing together what had happened to Rob.

Even though we were losing the light, we were able to carry out a preliminary search to satisfy ourselves that there was nothing obvious, and that he was not there, but could not be 100 per cent sure that there were no clues or smaller items to be found.

On return to the police station, I rang the leader of Milton Keynes Search and Rescue Team.

I gave him a full briefing, asking him to search the area surrounding the lake, with a particular focus on the area surrounding the large reed bed.

Meanwhile, I started looking ahead and creating a more detailed search plan. I already had well-trained search personnel involved, but after the obvious searches, what came next?

I needed to start planning for activities that would take place over the weekend. What searches should take place, what personnel were required and, importantly, was there anything else that could have happened to Rob?

Was there anything that I had missed?

I was confident with the theory that he'd gone into the lake and didn't think that anything *had* been missed. But in policing, just thinking that wasn't enough. What did we need to do to support or negate that theory? What were the risk points?

Based on what we knew from the witnesses, his likely direction of travel was towards the nearest end of the lake that was surrounded by a mass of tightly knitted reed beds.

If he'd gone into the lake at one of those points, he could be tangled up in there, so we'd need a more detailed search of that terrain in daylight. There were banks and paths to be scoured and on the other side of the lake, coves, gullies and a wooded area which would need a thorough search.

But I believed it was the reed beds that were key. Based on our theory, that was the most likely place we'd find Rob, so they were my absolute priority. I decided that we should use the police underwater search team to go into the lake, but the final decision to call them out would depend on what was found in the land searches, and would be made by the duty supervisors over the weekend.

My weekend off was approaching and I knew that I wasn't due back in for a couple of days. Despite this, I really wanted to work the Saturday to ensure that the investigation continued in the way that I wanted, so I spoke to the duty inspector.

'I'd like to work tomorrow, to oversee the search and continue the investigation,' I said. 'I want to be there.'

'You have to take your rostered days off, Charlie,' he said.

'Yes, but I started to get the investigation on track, and it has not been managed well thus far . . .' I protested.

'Leave a handover briefing for the duty sergeant tomorrow morning,' he said, 'It's nothing to do with you now.'

'But . . .' I started.

'It's your day off tomorrow and I'm not paying you overtime to come in,' he said firmly. His tone indicated that I didn't have a choice in the matter. The conversation was over.

It wasn't that I thought I was better than the team taking over. It was about continuity, something that hadn't been present in the investigation before my involvement, or for the family. I knew what needed to be done and I had a feel for the case. It felt like a big mistake not having me there.

But there was nothing to be done. I'd been given my orders.

Frustrated, I sat down to write a detailed briefing, ensuring that nothing was left out, as I did not want mistakes to be made.

The other action that was urgently required was for me to contact Rob's family. This was something that I had been thinking about since I had read the papers left for me but wanted to have something concrete to talk to them about.

Now that we had a plan, it was the right time.

It wasn't going to be an easy call, but it was an important one. I knew they were already feeling let down by the response and that I would have to find a way to build bridges with them and convince them that I was on their side.

As I dialled the number I'd been provided, I thought about what I was going to say. I wanted them to know that I was going to do my absolute best to find Rob.

But how could I promise to do my best, without providing false hope? The most I could do was offer a fresh start. My heart raced a little as the phone rang, then a man answered. It was the mother's partner, Darren.

'Sergeant Charlie Hedges here, I'm leading the investigation into Rob's disappearance now and I wanted to introduce myself,' I said. 'I know that things haven't gone as they should have done for you so far, and I want to apologise for that.

'We have had officers out making enquiries,' I explained. 'They found a witness who believes that he saw Rob not far from the lake that is close to The Sanctuary and CCTV confirms this. We have also conducted a search of the area, but not found anything of significance. I have organised a full search to take place tomorrow.'

'OK, that is good that you have some searches planned,' he said. 'He wouldn't have just gone off without telling anyone. It is not what he would do.'

'We are taking this seriously and will do everything we can to find him,' I said.

He replied, 'We are going to be there tomorrow and see the search. Will we see you there?'

'No, unfortunately not. It is my weekend off and I am not allowed to work, but my colleagues will be briefed to expect you and will explain what is happening.'

I had a further discussion with Darren about footwear that Rob would have been wearing and some other personal details to inform the search team. I wanted him to know that I had wanted to be there, but that not being possible, I'd put everything required into place.

While I understood the family's desire to be at the scene of the search, it wasn't ideal. Having family or members of the public turning up to assist searches could make things more complicated, given the delicate nature of such operations, but it was also difficult to say 'No, please don't do that' – especially when they'd been let down like Rob's family had.

Over the weekend, I did my best to put things to the back of my mind and get on with my days off, but every now and again it would creep in. *How were they getting on? Had they found anything? Had things progressed?*

I did hear snippets of information, a brief call here or there from colleagues. A pair of Rob's socks had been found in the wooded area. Then his shoe, floating in the lake.

A press release appealing for information was issued to local media, with the story being carried in local newspapers and on Horizon Radio.

So far, the findings of the investigation supported my theory that Rob had been close to the lake with the potential for having drowned. It wasn't the outcome that anyone wanted, but I hoped that they'd have a resolution before I was back on shift, or at least something that provided a solid clue to what had become of him.

By the time I returned to work the following Monday, nothing much had changed. I just had a much bigger pile of paperwork on my desk than I'd first been faced with. My stomach sank as I read through the notes. We were no closer.

My thoughts turned to Rob's family. I needed to contact them, to keep them informed and onside, but how would they be feeling about our lack of progress?

Devastated, frustrated, angry.

And rightfully so. They had been in Bletchley over the weekend, and I was confident that my officers had looked after them properly, but I wanted to reassure them that we would continue to look for Rob.

As their only assured point of contact, I knew I needed to speak to them. Their cooperation was important to the investigation. I updated them with our plans for further investigation and set a pattern for daily calls, sometimes several calls each day.

When I spoke to Laura, I was reminded of all the conversations I'd had when working in community policing, the knowledge that could be gleaned from understanding people's troubles and circumstances. I made sure to do what I knew to be important, and I listened.

It was clear to me that Laura didn't think Rob was off gallivanting. She thought something terrible had happened to her son.

'It's not like him, you know. I've told the other officers. Rob's not perfect and he likes to go out and have a good time,' she said. 'We are close, and he might not come home, but he would never do it without telling me.'

Through our conversations, I learned more about Rob and his family. She and Rob's dad had him when they were teenagers. One night, Rob's dad had gone for a night out with the boys and never came home. The next day it emerged that he'd been involved in a terrible accident and had been killed. He was nineteen.

The same age as Rob.

I recognised these elements from Rob's background as subtle indicators of his potential vulnerabilities, things that might influence his behaviour. They were not obvious things, like a physical or mental disability, but they did give vital context.

The story put further weight on Laura's adamance that Rob would not have just disappeared without telling her. Being close to his mum and knowing what had happened to his dad when he was the same age as him, why would he put her through this if he was just off having a good time? It didn't make sense.

The recovery of Rob's personal items had prompted the police helicopter to be sent up again and for search dogs to be taken to the site. But only a pack of his cigarettes had been found. The underwater search team had been called out as well and had turned up nothing at all.

I was perplexed; everything had pointed to Rob going into the lake. Finding nothing but a solitary shoe, a pair of socks and cigarettes of a brand that he smoked didn't make sense. But if the reed beds had been searched and nothing found, that negated my primary hypothesis.

Back in control of the investigation, I started to explore other possibilities. I recalled the underwater search team and asked them to search different parts of the lake, and arranged further searches by the police dogs, helicopter and search teams. But still nothing.

My officers were out making enquiries of anyone connected to activities around the lake and found out that a fishing match had been taking place, starting early on the morning that the rave had finished.

We contacted the organiser who was able to supply information about the participants, and they were traced, and statements taken, giving information about young males in the vicinity of the lake at relevant times.

Despite this, days had passed, and we were still looking.

The additional information and findings from our investigation, and our persistence, did mean that the case was finally being taken seriously and there was a strategic meeting with senior police officers to discuss our next steps.

I once again raised my conviction that there was no other rational explanation for Rob's disappearance being anything other than he had drowned in the lake, with the most likely point of entry into the water being the reed bed.

It was agreed that the underwater search team should make one further search of the lake. I had heard about a Lancashire police dog trained to locate bodies underwater and I asked that this same dog be used in our searches. My request was heeded and we arranged a day when we would have a final attempt to find Rob.

When I updated them, his family wanted to make the 200-mile trip to Milton Keynes once again, and I had arranged to meet them at the search site at 12.30 to take them through our next steps.

The searches commenced and I walked around monitoring the activity, watching one of the underwater search divers at a location further along the shore of the lake. He was wading purposefully towards a clump of reeds using his hands to feel below the surface for anything unusual. As I watched, my mind wandered.

What was it that we were missing? I puzzled.

There was no evidence of anyone else being involved. But why would he have gone to this part of the lake . . .?

Suddenly, an unusual movement by the diver interrupted my train of thought. He'd suddenly changed course and instead of wading towards the matted reeds, he was moving *away* from them.

What on earth is he doing? I thought.

I walked down to the bank of the lake and called out to him. He stopped in his tracks and looked up.

'Aren't you looking in the reeds?' I asked him.

'Oh no,' he said. 'It's really difficult to do that.'

'Pardon?' I replied, not quite believing what I was hearing.

'It's very difficult,' he repeated matter-of-factly. 'To search the reed beds. We don't do that.'

My mind started to spin. If they weren't searching in the reeds now, due to the difficulty, had they searched the main reed bed I'd indicated as the primary search area before I went on my rest days?

'What about the other reeds, in the other areas?' I asked. 'Were they searched?'

'Er, no,' he stuttered.

Anger bubbled inside, but I kept a cool head. I needed to challenge the search team about my concerns, but I needed to keep them onside too.

I was aware that in any crisis or emergency, shouting or anger could spark a similar response in others and was counter-productive. Remaining calm despite my feelings was imperative.

Was this a case of laziness, a lack of professionalism or a procedural failing?

They were all valid questions that needed to be answered, but understanding what had happened would have to wait – we needed to get the task in hand sorted out.

The frustration still simmered inside though. How could I explain this to Rob's family? It had been my main instruction. The one thing that I had indicated as a priority above everything else had been the reed beds. But they hadn't even been touched.

That location was close to where Rob's shoe and other belongings had been found. We still hadn't eliminated the possibility he was there.

I made my way over to the dive supervisor, 'Right, I want that reed bed properly searched. I've just been told it hasn't been searched. That it's too difficult to search. It is our primary search area, and it is imperative that it is done properly,' I said, controlling my anger. 'I am heading down there now, and I want to see that search being done.'

The supervisor just nodded, sensing now was not the time to argue with me. 'I'll get everyone back on it right now,' came the reply.

Within minutes, all the divers were pulled back to our initial focus point. They were at the end of the lake, working methodically through the reeds. My stomach churned in anticipation. After wondering what we'd missed, I was back to thinking I'd had it right from the start. They'd only been in the water thirty minutes when a solitary hand shot up in the air, belonging to a diver at the edge of the reed bed.

That was the sign used to indicate a find.

My heart raced as I watched events unfold; no words were necessary. My instinct told me that we'd found Rob.

They're probably thinking 'The old bugger was right about this' now, I thought, as the investigation team swung into action.

A few minutes later, my gut feeling was confirmed. A body had been found. From a professional perspective, I was pleased that I'd been proved right. But I was upset too. It was an incredibly sad moment. A young man had lost his life in tragic circumstances, the full extent of which we were yet to understand.

But another emotion returned too. Anger.

It was eleven days after he'd last been seen. Eleven days of unimaginable angst for Rob's family and friends. And it needn't have been that way.

Five days had passed since the first search was conducted and since I'd asked explicitly for those reed beds to be searched. While I doubted the outcome would have been any different, we could have had an answer sooner and minimised the distress caused by the burden of not knowing.

Leaving for my days off *had* been a huge mistake, that was for certain. If I'd been on duty, I would have seen the search wasn't being executed properly. I'd have sent the teams straight into the reeds and we'd have had our resolution five days ago.

There were no two ways about it. The job hadn't been done properly and a family had suffered because of it. It didn't really matter who dropped the ball and when – I was the investigation lead and felt the responsibility profoundly. The search was done, but my job was just starting, and I knew the next part was going to be incredibly difficult.

The knowledge weighed heavily on me, but there was no time to ruminate. The discovery had kicked another process into action: recovering the body, informing the family . . .

The family, I thought.

They were on their way to the site; it was now 12.10 and they were due to arrive in twenty minutes. The police helicopter was already circling above, and the divers were gathered in the area the body was located. By the time Laura and Darren arrived, the body could be being lifted from the water.

After everything they'd been through, that was the last thing I wanted them to see. It would just be too distressing. But how the hell was I going to stop them from coming down?

If I called them and kept it vague and said, 'We've found something,' I knew they'd be right down. I needed to give them reason to be elsewhere. Somewhere I could break the news gently.

Then I remembered, a shirt had been brought to us by a member of the public, an older woman who had seen the media coverage and turned up with a shirt that she'd found in a nearby hedge. It was a blue Moschino shirt that matched the description of what Rob had been wearing that night at The Sanctuary and earlier confirmed by the family to be similar.

47

I quickly pulled out my mobile phone and dialled Laura's number. She answered almost immediately.

'Hello, Laura, it's Charlie,' I said. 'The shirt I mentioned to you must be identified. Can you come to the station to identify it, so that we're positive?' I asked.

'Of course,' she replied.

After I hung up, I heaved a sigh of relief before climbing into my car. I didn't really want to leave the investigation at such a critical stage again, but there were people of sufficient rank and authority to oversee the recovery. Plus, I wanted to make sure the news was delivered properly.

As a police officer, delivering bad news to people was par for the course. But usually, your interaction with the family was a one-off, you were just a messenger. You hadn't sat with them and seen their angst, their hope, their anger.

Since I had been back in charge, I'd spoken to Laura and Darren every day, sometimes two or three times. We had a relationship and I felt that they trusted me. Yet still, even in my tenure on the investigation, we'd messed up.

As I drove back to Milton Keynes Police Station, I felt an overwhelming sense of dread. It was different to any other time I'd had to deliver this kind of news and I was struggling to keep a lid on my own emotions. I tried to plan what to say to them.

What are the right words in this situation? I thought.

They could be etched indelibly in their minds for the rest of their lives, so I knew the words I chose mattered. I wanted to do the best for them, but I wasn't quite sure what that was. Minutes later, they stepped into the visitors' room at the police station. After a brief greeting, we sat down, and I showed them the shirt.

'Is this Rob's?' I asked.

48

'Yes, it is,' Laura replied.

'Thank you,' I replied. Then I paused.

'I'm really sorry, but I've got some bad news,' I said. 'I've just got back from the lake, and we have found a body in the place that I thought Rob might have entered the water. There's no formal identification at the moment, but in all probability, it is Rob.'

They were obviously deeply upset, and they began to comfort one another.

'I am so, so sorry,' I said, my voice wavering, as I left the room to give them some privacy.

Even though I'd delivered this type of news a hundred times before, it had never felt like this. I also knew that whatever upset I was feeling, it paled in comparison to the agony Laura and Darren were going through.

I knew that a storm of emotions was churning beneath the surface. Pain and grief at losing a son, anger at the incompetence they'd experienced. I had no doubt they had questions too; why had it taken us so long to find him? If people had acted more quickly, would he still be alive? How had it happened?

Despite their obvious heartbreak, Laura and Darren remained calm and dignified.

'What happens next?' Darren asked.

'We need to go through some processes to verify that it is him,' I explained. 'There will be a formal identification, which I may need to ask you to be involved in.'

'Could we have some time on our own and is it OK if we have a smoke?' Darren asked.

'Yes', I said, 'that is fine. I will be back in a little while.'

It gave me the opportunity to ring Geoff White, the coroner's officer, a lovely man whom I had been a dog handler with.

49

'Hi, Geoff. The family want to identify the body and I wasn't sure if that's possible. Can you come and speak to them, please?'

'Yes, sure. I am just about to leave the lake anyway and will be with you soon.'

On my way back to the interview room, I was told off for allowing smoking in a non-smoking building. I did not really care though. It was the least we could do in the circumstances.

When Geoff arrived, I left the family with him, knowing I could trust him to take care of them while I returned to the lake. We might have found him, but the investigation wasn't over, and I was determined to get the answers that I knew Rob's family would so badly need.

The following day, Rob was identified by his family and his body was sent for post-mortem examination and toxicology, to determine the cause of death. I knew the toxicology samples would be critical to understanding what happened, but getting the results took weeks.

As we waited, we continued following up other leads. I'd been working from eight in the morning until midnight most days, using any resources I could find in the absence of an allocated investigation team – it just didn't exist for missing persons.

My team at Bletchley had been outstanding throughout, always rising to any challenge I gave them and working hard to achieve the objectives I set. But I had found throughout that every time I tried to move forward, any good work was undone by others simply doing what they had always done. It made me recognise that things needed to change.

Given the circumstances of what had happened to Rob, there was nothing the police could have done to have saved him, as information about his going missing was not known for some time after his disappearance. I knew we wouldn't ever have brought Rob home alive, but I still wasn't satisfied with the outcome. There were too many unanswered questions. How had Rob met his death? Parts of the story just did not seem to fit.

We'd been following leads connected to the friend that Rob had travelled down with. Through them it emerged that one of his friends had admitted to supplying him with ecstasy. He'd shown up in various command and control messages, where he'd contacted the police paranoid, saying he was being chased by people. Then there were witnesses saying they'd seen their car parked near the club, with the key on the bonnet.

The enquiries with the fishermen around the lake progressed, and some of them confirmed that they had seen two young males in different locations around the lake. One matched Rob's description and the other matched the friend he had travelled down with. The friend's credit card was also eventually found in the search area.

Was it just an accident or had something more sinister happened? Had there been an altercation? A dispute over the drugs?

Finally, the toxicology results arrived. As I read them, my jaw dropped.

They were negative. There was no sign that Rob had taken ecstasy.

I was baffled. We knew Rob had been supplied with the drug. Witness accounts of his behaviour indicated drug use. So, what *had* happened?

We needed to make sense of it. I wrote a report

concluding that we could not satisfactorily resolve the case based on the results of our investigations to date and timed it to land on several key senior officers' desks at the same time. As the potential for foul play needed to be explained, as well as the negative toxicology results, an incident room under the supervision of a senior investigating officer from the force's major crime team was set up.

I remained involved and we amassed a lot of additional detail about what happened on the night Rob disappeared, locating the person who'd supplied Rob's friend with the drugs in Cardiff. Arrests were made, including one on suspicion of homicide.

During the ongoing investigation, Rob's family spoke to a local newspaper, *Milton Keynes on Sunday*. When a copy landed on my desk, I was shocked.

Community ripped apart by 'murder' screamed the headline.

I didn't entirely disagree with Darren's summary that the investigation had been 'a total botch-up', but I certainly found some of the other comments difficult.

A 'lack of interest' in investigating Rob's death, being dealt with in a 'callous' manner by police and not being kept informed of developments.

There *had* been many mistakes, but once I was involved, I had done my very best to support the family. I was still trying my best to get a resolution.

Had I really got it as wrong as this article suggested?

As difficult as it was to read, I did understand. The family was grieving and angry and they had a right to their feelings on the matter. What was more concerning to me was a piece of information in the middle of the article, in a paragraph about some proactive action the family had taken during the search for Rob.

'They have travelled to the city with posters, interviewed witnesses who heard Rob being chased and screaming for his life, handing all the information to the police,' it read.

It was the first I had heard of such a sighting, and I knew it could be vital to the ongoing investigation, so I picked up the phone to the family immediately to get more information. Speaking to them was difficult, now knowing just how poorly they viewed the investigation, but I couldn't let my own feelings get in the way of finding the answers the family needed.

I was ready to pick up the new lead, but when I spoke to Darren, he was as surprised as me.

'We honestly don't know where that came from,' he said.

There was no witness who had seen Rob being chased and screaming for his life. Somewhere along the line there had obviously been some confusion, or perhaps a little journalistic licence. In the end, there wasn't enough evidence to prosecute anyone in relation to causing Rob's death.

I was devastated. Despite all the information we had, we still couldn't answer the question of what happened to Rob. I'd never be able to give the family the closure they needed.

I couldn't change that, and the thought haunted me. But there was something I could do.

I could examine exactly what went wrong with the police response, so no other family ever had to endure what Rob's did.

I began to compile a report. Our first failing had been the slow response. Assuming Rob wasn't vulnerable, that he was just a lad out having a good time, that had cost us time. By waiting, vital evidence may have been lost in those first few days – the 'golden hour' as it was known.

The 'golden hour' was the time immediately following an incident when there are the greatest opportunities for finding out what has happened and gathering evidence. The time when witnesses' memories were sharper and more reliable.

There was also the lack of recognition of the seriousness of missing person investigations. Our existing policy was woefully lacking, and in my lengthy report I highlighted what was wrong with it, what should be done to correct it and sent it to senior officers.

Several months after the investigation ended, Steve Flynn, who'd assigned the case to me, called me into his office.

'Charlie, I've got to serve these papers on you,' he said. 'It's your formal notice that Rob's family have made a complaint against you.'

I listened as he outlined the details: that I'd not spoken to them sympathetically and that a female officer hadn't been present when I'd broken the news to them.

I wasn't sure of what had prompted this complaint, and the comments that I hadn't been sympathetic when speaking to them surprised me. I'd struggled with the best way to break the news, acted to avoid them witnessing Rob being removed from the lake. I doubted my delivery was perfect, but had I really dealt with them so badly that they were focusing the complaint on me?

But I wasn't surprised at all they'd made a complaint about the investigation. I understood that the family was looking for accountability. In fact, had they asked me, I'd have actively encouraged it.

I completely respected their decision to challenge the force on its response to Rob's case. It had been a shambles.

And I was the investigation lead, so the responsibility fell on my shoulders.

All I could do was cooperate and get on with my job in the meantime. I knew that being investigated wasn't uncommon – in fact, it was expected. When I'd started out in the police cadets in Reading, a superintendent had explained the process to me.

'During the course of your career you will have to do things that people do not like, and I would expect to speak to you because someone has made a complaint against you,' he'd said. 'If I don't speak to you about a complaint then I am wondering why you're not doing your job.'

I knew I'd done my job to the best of my abilities in Rob's case, and I was happy to prove that. But more than that, I'd seen how much needed to improve around missing persons, and I wanted to be part of that change.

'Can you sort this out for me, Charlie?'

At the time I did not realise that that note from my inspector was the start of something that would change my life forever and develop my career in directions I never imagined.

I hadn't gone into the force with a focus on missing persons. I didn't have a particular specialism at all and my work with the police had been varied. What I did learn in the early days of my involvement, after Rob's case, was that there was very little understanding of what the implications of going missing really were.

It was common practice and sometimes policy that a report should not be taken for the first 24 to 48 hours because 'they always come back', whereas today's position is that a report should be made to police as soon as possible.

I had dealt with lots of missing person cases before Rob's case, but being consumed by one revealed a serious issue to me – the process of investigating a missing person was not up to scratch.

The police responsibility for missing persons has always been there, but guidance on how to respond was scant. There was an operational inertia around it, as the vast majority did just turn up.

'*Oh, they will come back,*' was a common refrain when a misper landed on an officer's desk.

The challenge was how to improve the process. Would improvement come through changing policies, or was there more to it? What about attitudes? Was there a true understanding of what a missing person was and what it meant?

Did officers know how to identify cases like Rob's, which needed a higher level of response, from the mass of other cases? Were there any new or improved procedures or responses that were needed? For me, Rob's case brought these questions to the fore, and many more emerged as time passed.

When the note asking to pick Rob's case up landed on my desk, I was vaguely aware of the case of sixteen-year-old Damien Nettles, who went missing on the Isle of Wight around a year earlier. The cases had similarities: slow police response, a mother not being listened to, the assumption that as a young man he was likely to be off having fun and that he'd turn up eventually. But Damien has never been found.

Experiencing the complaint from Rob's family was difficult, but it was yet another important lesson for me. While their complaint was justified, given what happened with the case, complaints would come even when you were doing things properly. People get upset and lash out because they have been caught doing something they shouldn't, or because they don't like authority, something that has happened several times during my career, with not one of those complaints proven to be justified.

Policing is a tough and often confrontational job and raising your head above the parapet and doing the right thing sometimes puts you in the firing line. It's an occupational hazard and one that it is important not to dwell on.

Reflecting on everything that had happened, there was nothing to indicate that officers deviated from what was the accepted way of doing things at the time, and that was the problem.

The phenomena of people going missing was not really understood, which led to a more casual approach than should have been applied. Policies and procedures were written with this ethos at their heart and so lacked the detail and focus that was really required to find those who were missing.

I had truly hoped that the changes I suggested would put an end to the fundamental mistakes that had been made. But as Damien's case showed, the issue was more widespread than I first thought. I was soon to learn that lasting change in the field of missing persons wasn't going to be easy to bring about.

CHAPTER 4

Unknown

Do you have a belief that the person may not have the ability to interact safely with others or an unknown environment?

Six months later, I was on another late shift, reviewing the incidents that were live in my area, doing a more in-depth check on what was in the command and control log from the past few days, so I was fully up to speed.

One incident caught my eye: a report of an elderly man who had been reported missing a few days earlier. As I read the information that was on our system, I was struck by a sense of déjà vu. Once again, besides the missing person's report there was very little else in the way of detail.

The man was missing from home in a rural area on the outskirts of Bletchley. He was around eighty years old and living with dementia, with serious concerns raised about his ability to look after himself, ask for help or otherwise engage with people. Yet no one seemed to be doing anything proactive to find him. No one was trying to understand what had happened.

It was as if they were just waiting for him to miraculously turn up, even despite his obvious vulnerabilities.

I was horrified. We'd been here before, with Rob's case, and all the same mistakes were being made. I'd pointed out all the problems just a few short months earlier, yet nothing had been done differently.

But no matter how disappointed and angry I felt, I needed to be calm and professional. Applying what I had learned from the previous case, using my investigative skills, and doing my best to find out what had happened and make sure that the necessary steps were taken; this man deserved our greatest efforts.

It was becoming clear to me that missing persons were simply not properly understood and generally this did not appear to be a problem because the majority do return. The problem lay in identifying those who needed extra attention, especially when the risk was not immediately obvious.

As I scrolled through other incidents that had occurred in my area, considering where best to start my enquiries, I came across another report. A sighting of an elderly gentleman walking on a footpath not far from where the missing man lived, on the same day that he had been reported missing.

On returning home and reflecting on what they'd seen, the informant had become concerned for the man's welfare. They'd called the police and described the sighting, saying the man had looked lost and that they were worried about him.

I was aghast. A confused old man sighted in the vicinity of where the missing person lived, and no one had made any connection?

I picked up the phone to call the informant, to see if I could glean any further information. Unfortunately, they couldn't add much, but they were able to describe more clearly where he had been spotted and the direction in which he appeared to be travelling.

Next, I spoke to anyone I could find who knew the missing man. Just a few simple conversations revealed valuable details that had been lacking in the file. It turned out that he'd been brought up on a farm and in his more lucid moments referred to those days with fondness.

There was no information to say where he had gone after walking out of his house, so I had to consider the evidence I had and the possibilities that presented themselves. I understood that dementia caused people to regress to their past and believe that they were living in that period. They often tried to return to doing the things that they would have done at that time.

If living on a farm and being in the countryside was a fond memory, could he have headed out towards a similar environment?

The town where he lived was small and rural, with a few houses dotted here and there before opening out into vast fields. Taking the location of the sighting on the footpath, it suggested a possible direction of travel that was leading away from where the man lived.

Out towards the countryside.

I drove out to the area to see if I could find any witnesses, going door to door and asking if anyone had seen the man. Eventually, I reached a farmhouse, where I spoke to the farmer who lived there.

'I do recall seeing someone on the path on my land,' he said. 'Quite an elderly man.'

'Do you remember what time?' I asked.

It was around the same time reported by the other caller and all the other information he provided was consistent with the information we had.

With the timing, description and direction of travel all corroborating each other, I was reasonably confident that the person who had been sighted by both the caller and the farmer was our missing person.

I undertook an initial search, looking for anything obvious, focusing on the route indicated by what I had learned. The terrain was mainly footpaths and open fields, so I was looking for anything unusual that the naked eye could detect – an item of dropped property like a shoe or wallet, a shred of torn clothing on a gatepost – anything at all that seemed out of place that might be connected to the missing man and could indicate what had happened to him. While I was being as thorough as possible, I also had to avoid wading into areas too bullishly, as I knew that evidence could easily be destroyed if care was not taken.

When I found nothing out of the ordinary in the immediate area, I cast my eye further, noting buildings with outhouses and woodlands in the distance for the plan that I would need to formulate to extend the search, as the wider area was too big for me to search alone.

It might not have turned up any new or solid leads, but until I made those additional enquiries, there had not been a focus for any search activity. Now I had one, and a proper search was essential.

With the usual resource issues, it was always a challenge to get enough officers together to conduct an effective search, so I decided to call Milton Keynes Search and Rescue out.

In the UK, searches for a missing person were coordinated by the local police, but forces made use of a network of volunteer agencies to assist. These volunteers had specialist training in areas like mountain, lowland, water and cave rescue.

Truth be told, I'd much rather have trained volunteers who wanted to be there out on the job, than police officers with little to no training and who probably did not relish the idea of an open country search.

I spoke to Roger Waghorn, the search team manager. Based on the age and physical health of the man, the nature of the terrain and the amount of access he would have, we agreed the initial parameters for the search. This is always a challenging decision, with the thought ever-present, 'Could the person have gone just that little bit further?'

The team, who were all trained volunteers, combed the area, checking gardens, farm buildings, bushes and fields for any sign, all briefed clearly on the process if something was found: *protect the scene, contact the police search coordinator and await their instruction on what should be done next.*

But after several hours, nothing was found. Reviewing our search strategies and building on what we already knew, Roger and I identified several new areas of interest.

When planning and managing searches, the question 'Could the person be just over the boundary of the search area?' was always present.

I believed we needed to extend the boundaries further. My rationale was that the terrain was reasonably flat and easy to negotiate, and I knew that it was easy to under-estimate how far someone in this situation can travel – and there were some wooded areas where a person could easily be hidden.

I wanted to continue the search, but not everyone was of the same mind.

'Stand the search team down, Charlie,' I was instructed by my supervisor.

Neither Roger nor I were happy with the decision. Left to our own devices, we would have pushed further, but there was a chain of command.

Unlike Rob's case, where there had been media interest from the start, there was no appeal for information or members of the public out looking for him; it was just us. I knew that it was wrong to stop just there, but how could we change the situation?

In so many cases, missing persons were found just over the border of an initial search parameter.

'If we could just cover those new areas . . .' he said.

'I agree,' I replied tersely, jaw clenched. 'We need to go that little bit further.'

'I've got an idea,' Roger said. 'I'm running a training day on Sunday. We could base the training areas on those places we think need looking at.'

This was on the Friday and, while not ideal, it was the best we could do. I was conscious that we were losing vital time, but it was better than nothing.

So many of the same mistakes had been made before I'd taken ownership of the case. The slow response, missing the 'golden hour', the lack of connection with other reports that had been received, the lack of understanding of how to resolve the case.

Just another misper . . .

My main concern was for the man and his family, but I was also aware this was indicative again of how things needed to change.

The investigation into the handling of Rob's case was still ongoing. The detective inspector assigned to it seemed to really understand the organisational failures that had occurred and was encouraging me to go on the record about it.

In a way, I felt that I already had. I had pointed out these failures in the report I wrote six months earlier and was furious that my warning hadn't been heeded, that my recommendations hadn't been implemented. If they had been, we wouldn't be in this situation, that was for sure.

As planned, the search got under way early on the Sunday morning, which was my rest day. It just so happened that I was travelling along the M1 Motorway adjacent to the search area when my phone rang. It was Roger.

'We've found him,' he said. I knew immediately from his tone that the news wasn't good.

'Where was he?' I asked.

'In the wooded area we identified,' he said. 'Tangled in some brambles.'

The poor man had passed away, alone in those woods. A person not suffering from dementia might have recognised the danger, realised the brambles were too thick to pass through, but he'd not been able to understand the risk. He'd just continued and become more entangled to the point he was unable to extricate himself.

'Thank you for letting me know,' I said. 'And thank the team for their work.'

I called the station to inform my colleagues and ask them to make the arrangements that were needed in relation to recovering and identifying the body and notifying people known to the man. It was a terrible outcome, but at least this time there was a clear explanation for what happened. There wouldn't be the unanswered questions that Rob's family had to live with.

Not that it would make losing a loved one any easier.

As I continued about my day, thoughts spun around my head. What would have happened if the initial response had been faster? What if we'd been allowed to continue our search rather than having to wait for days?

It was complicated but, potentially, a faster response might have meant that he could have been found sooner with the possibility of finding him alive.

When I returned to duty a couple of days later, I was still feeling angry. Rather than heading to my desk, I went straight to see my area commander, John Reeve.

I didn't wait to be invited to sit down. I needed to say my piece.

'Did you see this missing person case last week?' I asked.

'The elderly guy? Yes, I saw the job,' he replied.

'Sir, I sent you a report; I've identified the problems with missing persons and we're just doing the same things again,' I said. 'Why are we still getting it wrong?'

'Charlie, I understand that you're angry, but you need to learn something,' he said. 'Writing a report does not cut it. If you want to make a difference you have to get off your arse and do something about it,' he said.

I let the words sink in, and I realised he was right.

Right now, my report was just a piece of paper. I had to get leadership buy-in for my ideas. I had to get the policymakers in the organisation on board and the wider force to understand it was an issue. It was a huge under-taking, but it needed to be done. However much of an inconvenience they were considered, missing persons cases needed to be dealt with better. The missing people, their families, they all deserved better.

I was willing to take on the challenge, even though I had very little idea how to start, but I had to take responsibility for creating change. I realised now that writing reports did not make a tangible difference – you had to get on and make that change happen.

It was a little like starting an investigation; what did we already know? We had a local missing persons policy for

Milton Keynes, and I found out that a force-wide review of our missing persons policy was already being worked on and about to be introduced. I found the report and it was not fit for purpose.

They've not experienced these cases as I did and there was so much more to learn.

You could tell the policy had been written in the style of 'doing things the way they had always been done'. There was a need to have more dialogue with colleagues, other agencies, anyone else with knowledge of the subject. We needed to think outside of the box and do things differently.

It was a scary position to be in and not what I was used to, but it was important that changes were made, even if it was going to cause upset.

I lobbied everyone in relevant roles at leadership level to revise the policy on missing persons, raising my concerns. This got the attention of the superintendent who was ultimately responsible for the policy. She asked to see me and wanted to hear what I had to say. After our meeting, she arranged that I should work with her to conduct a full review and make those changes.

As we got to work, I had a clear vision. I wanted to move dealing with missing persons away from being a paper exercise and turn it into something more constructive and active. Even the language in the existing policy was static, talking about reports, just filling out a piece of paper. Simply changing the language to a 'missing person investigation' transformed the required action. It became something you had to go out and do, rather than something you just wrote down.

Driven to go out and speak to family, friends and witnesses, and really listening, officers would gather vital information, discover context and understand the full extent of the situation, like Rob's mum's adamance that his behaviour was out of character, or the information we received about the elderly man's dementia and his fond recollections of his old farm.

As the policy was implemented there was a gradual shift. Rather than just following a process – fill the form in and move on – people started to question what they were doing. It started a conversation about missing persons that didn't exist before. For the first time since Rob's case had landed on my desk, I felt like my concerns had been heard and acted upon.

Despite what felt like a small victory, at that point in late 1998 I started to struggle with an unfamiliar sensation. I was finding the simplest situations extremely stressful, with any challenge accompanied by unbearable feelings of inadequacy and anger.

It was subtle at first, moments when I felt I couldn't quite hide my irritation, or flashes of irrational anger at times when I'd usually be able to keep a cool head. Things like someone barging into me in the street when I was off duty, or not being able to find something when I was shopping.

All these simple day-to-day occurrences aroused an unreasonable feeling of anger and frustration.

This isn't right, this isn't me, I thought.

The instances started to become more and more frequent. Whenever I felt inadequate, or like people weren't paying attention to me, the anger came again.

It was an ordinary day and an ordinary shift when I realised something was really wrong. I arrived for duty, but even before the day had started, it was already there: a completely unwarranted anger churning in the pit of my stomach, threatening to explode.

As I sat at my desk, a new emotion collided with it. Distress. What the hell was wrong with me? Absolutely nothing had happened to provoke it.

The only thing that I did know for certain was that I was on the verge of reacting unreasonably.

Possibly even violently.

This was an unacceptable state for anyone to be in. But a police sergeant? I knew it wasn't safe for me to be on duty.

I went in search of my fellow sergeant, Gill.

'Gill, I need to go home,' I started. 'I've not been feeling . . . myself.'

I paused as I considered how to communicate what I was experiencing, given that I didn't really understand it myself.

'I've been feeling angry – very angry – for no real reason and I'm struggling to control it,' I explained. 'I'm not quite sure what's going on, but I know it's not appropriate for me to be in work. I don't think it is safe for me to be here.'

Gill listened and nodded. 'OK, Charlie, I'll cover for you,' she said. 'You just go home and get yourself sorted out.'

I was glad it was Gill on duty. She was approachable and we'd worked together on lots of things. Instead of probing, she listened. Maybe she read something in me and how I was acting. Or maybe she just knew me and accepted that if I was telling her there was a problem, there was a problem.

A huge weight lifted. After leaving work, I made a doctor's appointment. I decided the best course of action was to speak to him about how I was feeling, so I could try and tackle whatever the problem was.

He scribbled a note, signing me off and prescribing Prozac to help manage my symptoms. He had diagnosed 'anxiety state', a transitory emotional state consisting of feelings of apprehension, nervousness and physiological responses that I immediately recognised in myself.

'It's a normal reaction when you face a stressful or frightening situation,' he explained. 'It could be linked to your job.'

Things started to make sense. Throughout my career, I'd worked in a tough, stressful environment, dealing with road accidents, violence, death and abuse during my most mundane working days. It was so ordinary to me at that point that I hadn't even recognised its impact.

To support my recovery, I was provided counselling by the police. As we delved into the causes during our sessions, the possible triggers became more apparent. Rob's case was an obvious one, particularly with the protracted disciplinary enquiry that was still hanging over me, but there were other things too. Away from the 'normal' police work stresses, there were specific incidents from the past that I'd locked away, which had gradually been turning up the pressure. Like my colleague Alan's suicide. I'd considered it a tragic incident that had been dealt with, but counselling encouraged me to examine the real impact.

As I talked through it, I remembered how I had volunteered to take responsibility to inform a colleague who was close to Alan about what had happened. Our switchboard operator, Eileen (we all affectionately called her 'Aunty Eileen', as she'd been in the control room probably since before the world started) took good care of us all.

It happened on her day off, so I drove to her home to tell her the bad news. I knocked at her door, and she invited me in, completely unaware of what was coming.

'I'm really sorry, Eileen, I have some bad news in relation to Alan,' I'd said. Her face had dropped as I continued. 'Unfortunately, he was found dead at his house this morning.'

I'd explained the circumstances as best I could, allowing her time to take in the news.

'Did you see him beforehand?' she asked.

Eileen knew the shift rota like the back of her hand, so she knew that Alan would have handed over to me the night before he'd taken his life. It was a simple question, but it had flipped a switch in me.

Was there something I could have done about it? What had I missed?

'Yes,' I had said, my voice cracking as I tried to maintain my composure. But I couldn't.

Completely uncharacteristically, I had broken down in tears, standing in Eileen's hallway. Before I knew it, she was comforting me. I remembered feeling like I was failing in my duty.

I was supposed to be comforting her.

Looking back, I could see that this was the shock, the wondering what I'd missed, and the grief manifesting; they were all valid emotions. But at the time I hadn't thought they were appropriate. I was a police officer. Nothing was meant to touch me, and I was supposed to be able to deal with everything.

It was the first of many cracks in the wall I'd built up around me, like the incident with another colleague who murdered his wife and took his own life. I hadn't realised it, but all the trauma of learning about what happened, worrying about what I'd missed and the ways I might have failed — I'd carried it all with me for years.

Rather than dealing with it, I'd just locked it away and pushed on. I had done the same throughout my career, with difficult cases, work issues and problems in my personal life. Locking the emotions away and moving on – or so I thought.

But all the while I'd become a human pressure cooker, internalising my emotions and keeping a tight lid on them.

It wasn't just tough cases or tragic occurrences either. It was in the blurred lines between my professional and social life, like when my friend and fellow sergeant and I had gone for the same position as sergeant on the dog section.

Simon and I both desperately wanted this job, and despite being great friends, we were intensely competitive.

When Simon was selected over me, I was enormously disappointed.

When I'd arrived at his leaving celebration, the venue had been heaving, with loud music and a lively melee of people jostling to get to the bar. Slipping into a gap, I'd waited patiently, observing the staff flitting from customer to customer. Then I'd noticed a man who'd appeared from nowhere and immediately caught the bartender's attention.

As I watched him make his order, the same sensation that had become more frequent had washed over me. I'd been irritated that he'd jumped the queue. But looking back, it had been far more than that. I'd begun to feel twitchy and agitated.

Was I so inadequate that I couldn't even get a drink? Was I invisible? I'd thought.

As quickly as the thought came, I'd tried to talk some sense into myself.

What was I thinking? Why was I reacting like this? I thought.

It was just a drink, after all. I was a calm person. Even in highly charged environments and situations I'd always remained level. But then the sensation churned again, my internal monologue mocking me.

'Look at you. Failing to complete the simple task of buying a drink.'

It was like I was goading myself, and it was working. Anger churning in the pit of my stomach, I clenched my teeth and gripped my wallet, trying to force the feeling away. But it pushed back, building up more intensely each time I tried to dismiss it. As I'd struggled to maintain control, panic began to rise inside me. The noise, the bodies in the room, everything seemed to be closing in.

'What's going on?' I'd thought. *'This isn't me.'*

I'd stepped away from the bar, having finally managed to buy a round of drinks, and found a quieter space to collect myself.

'You all right, Charlie?' a colleague asked.

'Yes, yes, fine,' I'd said, as breezily as I could muster. But I was anything but.

I'd tried to make small talk with colleagues, but even away from the bar the churning emotions didn't quiet. Everything had seemed to be blowing out of proportion; the room felt louder, busier, more confined. Every laugh and glance seemed amplified, prodding what felt like an unruly beast trapped inside me.

I had no idea what was going on. I couldn't hear. I had no room to think, and the pressure was just building up and up and up. I knew I couldn't stay.

'I'm sorry, I'm not sure what's up with me, but I need to not be here,' I'd announced to a colleague I'd been trying to hold a conversation with.

'Ah, come on, Charlie, you're just jealous of Simon,' he'd teased, as I started to walk towards the door.

It was intended as banter, but I'd known in that moment that if I stopped to engage, I would have ended up doing something outrageous. So I left.

That night, I had felt like a stranger in my own body. The person at that party hadn't felt like me and he didn't react like me. I'd had no idea who he was, and I'd certainly hoped he wasn't going to return.

But now, with the benefit of hindsight and armed with the knowledge I'd gained from my doctor and my counselling, I understood. All those feelings and reactions had been signs, a build-up of stress, frustration, sadness, anger – a whole range of emotions that I'd internalised over years – finally escaping.

No matter how hard I tried, they weren't going to go away. I had to let them out and learn how to deal with them.

Being signed off work was an enormous relief, but it left me with an abundance of time on my hands. My counselling, which took place in Oxford, occupied an important proportion of it, but I couldn't just spend the rest of my time at home. If I'd been physically sick, I might have been confined to my bed and had no choice in the matter, but dealing with a mental issue was different and I had a choice.

I'd never been the type to sit around and watch daytime television, it just wasn't me. So, free from work commitments and schedules, I fell back on the outdoors, spending hours in the countryside of North Buckinghamshire, walking or on my bicycle, absorbing the scenery and wildlife. My time outdoors now had a vital restorative role.

The fact that my illness wasn't physical came with a palpable sense of guilt.

I felt weak and inadequate, and the whole situation – why it had happened, why I was so incapacitated by it – was a mystery to me. The police force wasn't really an environment where mental health issues were recognised and talked about by the majority, which didn't help.

I didn't have a huge circle of friends and did not feel I wanted to share what was happening with them anyway. My family lived some distance away and this was not something that I really wanted to burden them with. So, outside of my sessions, I was limited with whom I could talk to, but that was OK, as I had always been a self-sufficient person, used to finding solutions to problems.

As the weeks passed, the heaviness slowly started to lift. I always looked forward to my counselling sessions.

My counsellor would send me away with homework, relaxation and meditation tapes to quiet my mind. I'd realised that I was constantly living as though a bomb had exploded in my head, shards of information and emotion always whizzing around. I had constantly been measuring my professional environment, wondering what I should or shouldn't say and fighting to filter my thoughts appropriately. Those thoughts and processes were all clogged up in my head.

Gradually though, I was able to unpick the issues, find clarity and create some peace for myself. I found myself inspired by how my counsellor worked. I knew that many of the things we discussed were difficult and upsetting. Yet, as each session ended and we said our goodbyes, I'd walk towards the door and watch her as she closed her eyes, sitting there calmly and processing the session.

She was visibly allowing my burden to roll off her, picking everything I'd told her up and putting it to one side. She was there to help me, but not to take on my burden. As much as our conversations were vital, seeing how she managed was a lesson for me too. It made me realise that I needed to do the same in my professional life. I could do my job, make a difference, without taking it all on personally.

I felt a gradual shift, but the process was slow. One day I'd taken myself out to Milton Keynes shopping centre. I was emerging from a shop when out of nowhere, my area commander, Peter Hilton, appeared.

My heart sank immediately as an intense wave of guilt washed over me. Even though I was signed off sick, I felt like I was skiving when my colleagues were all working hard and inevitably picking up my slack.

I braced myself as Peter confronted me, sure that he'd have some words about me being out shopping when I was supposed to be ill.

'Hi, Charlie,' he said. 'You look dreadful. I can see why you shouldn't be at work.'

It sounds strange, but it was the nicest thing someone could have said to me. He didn't think I was skiving; he could see something in me that warranted me being off work. It was comforting for my issues to be seen in that way.

My colleagues weren't all like Peter though. Part-way through my leave, a supervisory officer visited me at home, as was protocol for those on long-term sick. It was immediately clear that he was uncomfortable and did not really understand what stress-related sickness was. Almost at once he turned the conversation to what was happening at work.

As he regaled news of cutbacks and officers being moved around to save money, my head began to swim. *Was I going to have a job to go back to?*

After he left, I tried to use the skills I'd learned in counselling to put the thought aside. It wasn't within my control, and it wouldn't help to dwell on it, so I just got on with my day.

Later that night, after being asleep for a few hours. I woke suddenly at around 2 a.m. I felt very strange, not physically, but mentally.

At first, I told myself it would pass.

Go back to sleep, don't be stupid, I thought.

But the disconcerting feeling stayed with me. Knowing that ignoring these feelings hadn't worked well for me in the past, I decided to get up and try and figure it out. But when I tried to move, nothing happened.

I could not work out how to get up; my brain wasn't processing what I needed to do. I was completely immobile. Fear gripped me and I felt panic rising in my chest.

What the hell was this? Was I physically incapacitated? Did I need to call an ambulance? Or was it my mind?

That's it, I've completely lost it now, I thought.

There was no chance I'd just go back to sleep. I was too scared. But I knew I couldn't just lie there and wait. I needed to find out if I was still capable of moving. I closed my eyes and tried to calm my mind, then I started to break down the process into single actions.

Sit up, Charlie.

Although my body felt like a lead weight, I heaved myself into a sitting position.

Now move your right leg.

I swung my right leg over the side of the bed and paused, taking a deep breath.

Now your left leg.

I continued my step-by-step process, walking across the room, opening the door, making my way down the stairs and through the stages of making a cup of tea. It had taken an age, but I was relieved I'd been able to move.

Was I completely broken?

'This was your body's way of dealing with the chat with your supervisory officer, to avoid overload and protect itself,' my counsellor said at my appointment later that day.

It was a transient issue. My body's coping mechanism had kicked into gear and protected me by only allowing me to decide what to do in easy steps. As frightening as it had been, it was a revelation to understand the connection between my body and mind.

Before long, my counsellor discharged me.

'You don't need me any more, Charlie,' she said. 'You can go and do this on your own.'

The culture in the police at the time was one of 'get on with it and don't talk about it', apart from dark humour and banter at the end of the shift. I think at the time, we all thought that was enough. Looking back, I can now clearly see the individual matters that didn't cause me conscious concern at the time, but slowly and cumulatively built up, in the absence of any outlet for talking about and dealing with them.

While the support I received from the police – my leave of absence, the counselling and time at a convalescent home – was good, it had only been available at crisis point.

It was a tough way to learn the lesson, but this is where I found that hiding your feelings and concerns and bottling it up just does not work. I also realised that you do not have to take on the burden of a difficult situation to help fix it. You can be empathetic and care, you can support people, but you don't own the problems. This understanding has been vital throughout my career, and it is something I frequently remind myself and others of. The understanding of mental health in the police has come on a lot since my time. The pressures of the job are still there but there's better consideration of mental wellbeing and employees' welfare issues. There's more access to support and counselling at early stages, but I am sure the 'man up and get on with it' attitude still exists in some areas. It's important to keep maintaining the message that being impacted by the work and needing help isn't a weakness.

Since learning these lessons, and better understanding mental health issues, I've felt mentally stronger and far more capable. I am often asked how I manage to cope when dealing with the horrific things my work presents me with, like the things that happen to children related to going missing. The answer is that I focus on improving things, finding ways to better understand those situations and implement solutions.

I cope because I believe that what I do creates better outcomes.

To this day, many of my coping mechanisms still involve the outdoors. I realise now that physical activity and the connection with nature that my family – my mum in particular – instilled in me is what we now call mindfulness.

I've learned that no matter how big, complex or over-whelming a situation is, all you can do is just get to the end of the day and consider the next one, being mindful of the things you can control and those that you can't.

When things are difficult, not going well or tough decisions must be made, I also turn to the Serenity Prayer. It is something that gives me balance in my life and a sense of proportion. It enables me to step back and take stock to consider what I can or cannot do.

> *God grant me the serenity*
> *to accept the things I cannot change;*
> *courage to change the things I can;*
> *and wisdom to know the difference.*

Mind you, I do not always accept the things I cannot change. Some things are worth fighting for.

CHAPTER 5

Trafficked

Could they be a victim of sexual exploitation?

Although I had been careful to take things one step at a time on my return to work, it wasn't long before I spotted an opportunity I couldn't miss to further my desire to improve the police response to missing person cases. I was reading a police magazine when I found a flyer for the Police Research Award Scheme (PRAS), funded by the Home Office to develop innovative ideas that could benefit policing.

It was an ideal platform to highlight and explore the use of important behavioural information to locate the missing.

'If you want to make a difference you have to get off your arse and do something about it.'

This was an opportunity to share my ideas on a national and force-wide level. It would allow me to undertake proper research and develop something that might have an impact.

I decided it was worth a shot, without holding out too much hope. The deputy chief constable, Paul West, liked the idea but didn't think my application was strong enough.

'I'm going to ask Rob Oxley, my staff officer, to work with you on refining it before it's submitted,' he said.

After feeling so unheard on the matter, I was absolutely bowled over by the level of support being offered to me.

My reworked application was successful, and I was awarded a grant to carry out the project, which had the working title 'Locating Missing People Using Behavioural Information'.

My peers on the scheme were working on a wide range of subjects, like a firearms officer who was studying the effect of a bullet going through glass. A couple of others had many similarities with my own project. One was led by an officer from Grampian Police and an experienced mountain rescue search manager. His name was Graham Gibb, and he was looking into the time and distances travelled by missing persons according to their age, gender, health and the reasons for going missing.

Where my work focused on behavioural implications, like why they went missing, their patterns of behaviour and what happened to them while they were away, Graham's focused on geographical and spatial data. I quickly realised that there was a lot to share with and learn from one another.

Working with forward-thinking and like-minded people, who cared as much about the field of the missing as I did, was a huge boost. After such a difficult time, I didn't just feel mentally stronger – my drive to improve attitudes and responses to missing people was reinvigorated. With the opportunity in my hands, I was determined to make a difference.

The harsh realities of research for my PRAS project very quickly kicked in. As I started accessing missing persons reports going back over several years, the true scale of the challenge became apparent. Held entirely as paper documents, I was shocked to discover just how little detail was recorded on reports and it only served to reinforce my view that missing persons were not dealt with effectively nationally.

When considering what might be relevant when investigating a missing person case, I identified the fact that vital information was often absent from reports: illness, occupation, truancy from school, previous occasions reported missing, transport that was used or available to the misper, circumstances while away, even the circumstances of going missing.

I could see that there was a bigger and much more important piece of work to be done, so I contacted the Home Office to discuss my concerns. Based on the information I presented to them, they agreed to allow me to shift my focus towards reviewing all aspects of missing persons and develop recommendations for the whole of the UK police.

Of course, this work had to be undertaken alongside my very busy and challenging day job managing the busy operations department at Milton Keynes, which was responsible for planning and resourcing major commitments, major operations and critical incidents. Some of these were planned, like regular 60,000-capacity concerts at the Milton Keynes Bowl, while others we had to respond to as they developed, like the fuel protests of 2000.

We had a tight and experienced team, with expertise in traffic management, self-defence, conflict resolution and search and rescue, while I had the autonomy to be in charge of my own and my team's destiny. I was trusted to get on with the job, do it in my own way and work the hours that were needed to achieve results.

But even with all that knowledge and experience, the pace of the job meant that sometimes things were missed. One day, I was in the operations room with Chief Superintendent Mick Page standing next to me, casting a critical eye over our work as we prepared for a sold-out Bon Jovi concert at Milton Keynes Bowl. Traffic controls were in place and there were around 100 officers on the ground. Everything was planned as normal, but some unusual traffic issues started to present themselves.

As I looked into them, my heart sank. There was another enormous music festival that we hadn't accounted for taking place 19 miles away from our event, causing conflicting traffic flows.

How on earth had I missed that?

I knew that if audiences were not in their places for the start of the concert, we'd have failed in our role, but at this stage all we could do was sit tight and hope for the best.

Sensing my tension, Mick took a step closer to me.

'It will be OK, won't it, Charlie?' he asked quietly.

All I could muster in response was a squeak, but by the skin of our teeth, it all worked out OK.

In fact, it was a valuable lesson in looking at the big picture and the fine detail, making sure nothing was missed and understanding how seemingly disparate events and incidents were connected, which was becoming equally important in my work on the PRAS programme.

Despite cynically thinking that my work on PRAS wouldn't elevate my visibility, I started to become known nationally as someone with a passion for missing persons. I was invited to join a national working group looking at missing person procedures, which was headed by the Association of Chief Police Officers (ACPO) lead, Commander Alan Shave from the Metropolitan Police.

At our meetings at the iconic New Scotland Yard building, I had to pinch myself for not being able to believe what I had moved on to. From the time when I had started to agitate about the inadequacies of how they were dealt with, to now, when I had been given the role as coordinator of missing persons, which meant having the oversight of all missing person cases within the Milton Keynes police area. Keen to fulfil this responsibility to the very best of my abilities, I invested considerable time into reviewing every single case, trying to fill gaps, improve processes and in some cases, join the dots.

In the course of this work, my attention was drawn to a situation that had been going on for some time in Bletchley. There were an unusually high number of missing persons reports coming from one estate, all of which were taking up a lot of police time, seemingly to no end.

When people returned, it was generally recommended that an officer was sent out to speak to the person, to find out if they had experienced any harm. But this didn't always happen, especially if the person frequently went missing. When these return interviews were conducted, it was often by whichever officer was available, rather than one who had been involved with the case. With no existing relationship in place and no trust built, the interviews rarely provided any insight.

'Nothing happened. I just stayed out longer than I should have.'

Each case on file was being dealt with individually and each was regarded as a nuisance.

The estate was one of the more deprived in the area, with poverty, addiction and antisocial behaviour creating plenty of issues. The parents of many of the young people who were going missing had their own difficulties and often a strained relationship with the police, so they were difficult to engage.

There had always been a problem with teenage kids going missing. They were the most prolific. The more troubled their home lives and extreme their difficulties – especially those who were living in care – the more regularly they went missing, some more than a hundred times.

As a parent, I was mindful of these issues and how they could become present in any family, even my own. My son Tom was now 10 years old and growing up fast, and I was confident he was on the right track and had two supportive, caring parents. But I understood how a less supportive environment could negatively impact children, and the considerable difficulties that could cause.

Some police had a less than favourable view of these individuals and their families. The lack of engagement, constant troubles and issues that surrounded them meant they didn't always see the point in continuing to try and help them.

But discarding these people, particularly the youngsters, just because they were underprivileged and lived in challenging circumstances didn't sit right with me. It wasn't their fault.

If these children were going missing, it wasn't for the fun of it. There had to be a reason.

With the common denominator of the estate as my basis, I started to look at them collectively.

Did they move in similar circles?

Were they known to one another?

Were the timings similar?

Other similarities soon presented themselves. The greatest volume of the reports involved teenage girls going missing. I could see the same addresses being mentioned in reports relating to different girls, as well as names of people reported to be in contact with them.

Clearly there were overlaps between the cases, but was there something that connected them directly?

Trying to get that answer was to prove challenging as across all the cases, none of the girls were talking to the police and the cooperation of their parents was limited.

I made some initial enquiries but they revealed nothing about what was happening. The insistence that they'd 'just stayed out longer than they should have' persisted.

The only additional information I unearthed was the fact that the times and dates on which they went missing and then returned were similar, along with a couple of seemingly unrelated addresses cropping up in some of the reports. Being met by a wall of silence was frustrating. In the other missing persons cases I'd worked on, people would have been willing to talk but they hadn't been asked.

I was still not seeing the whole picture. Then one day, I met a former colleague, Martin, who had left the police and was now working in the local children's services social work team. We hadn't seen one another for a while, but as we chatted, I mentioned the case of the missing girls and a few of their names, thinking he might have some insight.

'Oh yes, those names ring a bell,' he said.

The more we talked, the more it appeared that his team was dealing with the same girls as we were. Police and social services didn't tend to work together closely on the day-to-day, but it seemed to me that by working together, we might have information that one another could find useful.

'Do you think it might be useful to set up a meeting?' I suggested. 'We can share the information we have and see where that takes us.'

A few days later, I was in Milton Keynes council offices, where children's services were based, with all the information I had on the relevant cases for a meeting with Martin's team.

Lo and behold, his colleagues arrived at our meeting with another stack of additional information that wasn't present in police files. They had the same list of names and one of the social workers had even started a chart mapping out all the connections between them on a piece of paper.

Over the course of several meetings, I added my information to the chart – timings, relevant people and locations – and a pattern started to emerge.

The reason for children's services' involvement in each case was different; they were a member of a family of concern, antisocial behaviour or a tendency to go missing. But across all the cases, one name in particular cropped up too regularly to be ignored.

He was a male in his thirties and had been living in the nearby town of Northampton. A search of police records showed that he had come to the attention of Northamptonshire Police due to indications that he may have been trying to take advantage of young girls, probably for sexual purposes. Before a case could be built against him, he'd moved over the border to live in our area.

His name came up as a person many of the girls had been in contact with, and his car registration was showing up in key locations at times that aligned with when the girls were going missing.

I knew this was a breakthrough moment. It was obvious that this man was the common factor in the disappearances, the thing that I'd been looking for to connect all the dots. It was possible that he could be luring them into liaisons with other men. This gave me a better understanding of the reasons why they might have been unwilling to speak to us.

They might have been frightened of him or scared they'd get in trouble.

Armed with the new information, we were able to establish a pattern, whereby he was picking the girls up and taking them to different towns, then taking them home again, often leaving them with gifts that seemed out of proportion to what young girls should have on their person, such as amounts of cash, cigarettes and alcohol.

Something was clearly wrong with this situation. It was completely inappropriate behaviour to take place between an adult and young girls, and deeply concerning, given Northamptonshire Police's interest in the man. While we had information, there was a lack of evidence to support a criminal prosecution and the girls would not talk about what was happening.

I knew we had to remove this man from the equation. My hypothesis was that once he was off the scene, the girls would stop going missing.

We were going to have to be creative. I did some further research on the man. Through the national police database, I found that he was flagged as a disqualified driver, yet he was still using his car. I alerted patrols to the man, sharing his registration number and vehicle details, as well as the areas he frequented, and instructed them to look out for him.

The flouting of driving bans was something of a bugbear for police officers. For them, this was always 'game on' and an opportunity for payback to someone who obviously thought they were above the law. Cops would even sit quietly round the corner from the man's address, watching and waiting for him to drive off.

Whenever he was spotted out driving, he was pulled over and arrested. This happened so many times that the court eventually sent him to prison.

Sure enough, as soon as he was behind bars, the girls stopped going missing and dropped off the police radar. The immediate risk was removed, but the job was unfinished.

'We're still working with them, but they're not talking,' Martin said. 'We have nothing to go on.'

He was right, sadly. To take things further, we'd need the girls to make allegations of offences committed against them. Alternatively, we needed evidence of what was happening while the girls were missing, but this also required information from them which they weren't sharing. With no testimony to the contrary or evidence of any of these crimes, there was nothing more the police could do.

However, children's services did still have contact and provided safeguarding, and the fact that we now had an open channel of communication between our two organisations gave me some comfort and confidence. I knew that if one of the girls ever spoke out, they'd be straight back in touch, and we'd be able to work together to bring the man to justice.

The case showed to me that 'missing' in and of itself wasn't the issue, it was an indicator. It also highlighted just how important talking to other agencies was.

Knowledge and information sharing between the police and overlapping services was so rare. It wasn't just cross-departmental and local collaboration and cooperation that was the problem, either – it was the prioritisation of risk. The number of reports being made to the police regarding people going missing was in the hundreds of thousands per year, but there was only one assessment to ascertain if the missing person was vulnerable or not – and how it was interpreted and applied varied across forces.

The assessment was based largely on age and a few medical conditions, the presence of which would ensure they were recorded as missing. However, as with my experience with Rob and the gentleman with dementia, being acknowledged as vulnerable and recorded missing didn't necessarily mean such cases would be a priority.

I noticed some concerning 'myths' in police dealings with mispers as well, like 'they always come back'. This prompted the belief that missing person reports should not be taken until 24 or even 48 hours had elapsed since the person was last seen, allowing truly vulnerable people to slip through the net.

Another was that those who went missing on multiple occasions were less at risk because they were deemed 'streetwise', a term that I had come to abhor, particularly after dealing with the girls from Bletchley. They had been considered 'streetwise' by the virtue of their behaviour, attitude, confidence and demeanour. The term had come to suggest that they were not at risk because they were clever enough to look after themselves. However, the opposite was true. These young people were *more* at risk because of these factors. They were more likely to push boundaries and engage in risky behaviours, putting themselves in more danger.

The idea that our risk assessment system could be missing vulnerable people troubled me deeply. But I also knew that police response had to be proportionate. We needed a tool that would ensure we were not under-responding to serious cases, while not probing too deeply into someone's life when it was not justified, remembering that adults had a right to go missing if they wished.

As part of my PRAS I explored risk assessment models that were used inside and outside of the police. I found a number that were useful, including one I discovered through my work with specialist search teams.

It was called the 'urgency analysis' and was used by mountain rescue teams to determine how urgent the need for them to respond to a lost person was. Rather than just the basics about the person, the analysis looked at the individual, the environment in which they were lost, and their ability to survive in such conditions.

Markers included health: whether the person had a known or suspected injury or illness, were healthy or known to be a fatality (for example, if searching for someone who has fallen from a cliff whose height meant it would be impossible to survive the fall); equipment: inadequate, questionable or adequate for the known conditions; and terrain and hazards. These provided specific indicators of risk and I realised that the approach could be extremely useful in assessing risk in missing person cases.

The risk assessments used in the police gave *some* assessment of risk but were not quite fit for purpose. I was not convinced that they were sufficiently robust or accurate and there was no national standard, with forces using a range of different risk assessment models.

The UK's largest force, the Met, used a numerical weighting system, which meant assigning numbers to factors like age, health and family or work problems and creating a numerical banding system to indicate low, medium or high risk.

Low risk meant there was no apparent threat or danger to the subject of the report or the public. Medium risk meant the subject was likely to find themselves in danger or be a risk to themselves or others. High risk indicated an immediate risk and substantial grounds for believing the subject is in danger through their own vulnerability or mental state, or that the subject's mental state could place the public in danger.

The scoring system would allow officers to score each factor, add the numbers together and make it easier to prioritise the case. Officers loved it as it made their lives easier, but it was flawed.

There was no real science behind the numbers. Very young children obviously had a high score, but the score would differ between one day before and one day after a birthday.

We knew that life was not that defined. You didn't necessarily go to bed aged fifteen, then wake up the next day aged sixteen and suddenly be more mature and therefore less at risk. It also did not allow for varying abilities between people of the same age.

The numerical system might have been simple, but I could see that it wasn't effective. It wasn't the answer when it came to assessing risk.

Through my work I brought together the most useful and effective elements of all the models I had explored, developing a tool that was a decision-making guide rather than a simple assessment.

Removal of the numerical scoring wasn't popular with officers as it presented more work, but I was convinced it would improve outcomes in missing person cases.

As I continued to research my PRAS project, I began to meet and draw on the experience of charities that focused on the needs of missing people and their families, including the National Missing Persons Helpline. The charity was set up by two sisters, Mary Asprey and Janet Newman, following the case of Suzy Lamplugh, an estate agent who went missing in 1986. With the case never resolved, the charity switched its focus to supporting the families of missing people, in particular the long-term missing.

It was through the charity that I met Juliet Singer, one of their employees. Juliet specialised in human trafficking. My own knowledge around trafficking was in relation to drugs, not people, and it wasn't even from direct experience.

As a neighbourhood police officer, drugs trafficking was a few more rungs up the ladder from me. Departments with international remit would be investigating drugs being smuggled from Colombia and other places around the world into the UK, as part of a multi-million-pound underworld. After that it would be the local drug squads dealing with the dealers who distributed the product in their territories.

In my role, I would see the end result of drug trafficking, with young people involved in low-level drug dealing, addicts, street dealing and associated crime and violence. If we did get our sights on a key dealer, the case would be referred to the drug squad for them to investigate.

Through the knowledge I gleaned, I was starting to recognise that people could be substituted for drugs and become the commodity that was sold and exploited, and going missing could be an indicator for this.

Juliet and I were invited to attend a conference on trafficking at Interpol headquarters in Lyon, France, where one of the speakers was Detective Sergeant Paul Holmes from the Metropolitan Police. He was a leading expert in people trafficking and the horrific exploitation that accompanied it.

The room fell silent as he stood to give his presentation. He shuffled his notes, paused, then turned to his boss, an assistant commissioner who was in the audience.

'Sorry, ma'am, I am about to retire, and I am going to tell it as it is,' he said, discarding his notes.

In the highly regimented police world, it was a rather unprecedented move, and the room crackled with anticipation.

The idea that people were being smuggled was a very emergent concept. Paul had gone deeper than anyone to understand human trafficking and had dealt closely with the aftermath of it. It was clear that we were about to hear some harsh realities.

What followed was the most impassioned speech I'd ever heard. Paul described the true nature of people trafficking, the human suffering that resulted from exploitation that involved coercion, abuse, rape, imprisonment – all for the perpetrators to make huge amounts of money. The impact of this was felt in the UK, in every town, with girls being brought into the country and forced to provide whatever services – most often sex – that the traffickers wanted them to provide. He talked of young girls coerced or tricked into leaving their home country and taken to other countries, including the UK. They would be placed in appalling conditions and forced, sometimes through being beaten or raped, into complying with the will of their captors.

It was graphic, shocking and – judging by the silence in the room at his conclusion – had made an impact on everyone present.

He had put into words something that many of us were starting to see but didn't yet understand. These human traffickers were using the same methodology of drug smuggling and applying it to humans. It was a much lower-risk way of reaping the same rewards as high-level drug dealers involved in international operations.

If you were captured with a bundle of drugs in the back of your van, it would be hard to argue your guilt.

But caught with compliant human victims, who had been briefed on what to say and made aware of the horrific consequences if they did not, was a very different matter.

Being missing could easily be an indicator of these dreadful and sinister crimes. If we looked below the surface to find out why people were behaving in the way that they were, is this what we might find?

On my return to the UK, I asked if I could organise a seminar on human trafficking and invited Paul and Juliet to speak.

There was no intelligence to support it at the time, but intuitively, I knew it was happening everywhere, including in Milton Keynes and throughout the Thames Valley. I also knew that in the rank and file it either wasn't understood and recognised, or they saw it as a London-centric issue.

'That's not happening in my town,' was a common refrain.

'The Met are dealing with this on a daily basis, and it's going to be happening here,' I said.

There were about fifty people in the room, from patrol officers to supervisors and senior officers. I watched as both Paul and Juliet shared their professional experience and the gut-wrenching experiences of the victims of human trafficking.

This wasn't just a distant or imagined nightmare scenario, or an over-exaggeration, it was happening, right here and right now.

We had not advanced enough to be investigating such cases in my police area, but things I had learned started to take on a new meaning. A review of local advertisements for prostitutes had revealed a range of nationalities that matched those of the trafficked victims that were being found in London.

There were indications in cases I was dealing with too, like one young girl who was going missing repeatedly. We were working with her to try and figure out why this was happening, but she was reluctant to talk. When she did, she eventually confided in me that she was being controlled by a local criminal gang leader – an older man. The more information we gathered, the more the intelligence suggested trafficking was potentially an issue, but we were unable to make any progress because she was too frightened to make a formal complaint.

'I need to tell you, but if he knows I tell you, my life will be at risk,' she said.

I wasn't surprised. If she dared to try and escape the cycle she'd been pulled into, he'd talk to her about it with a gun in his hand. No amount of reassurance from the police or other agencies could convince her we could keep her safe.

It was a hard pill to swallow. As cops we were supposed to be the knights in shining armour who rush in to save everyone, but sometimes it was more complicated than that. By doing nothing I knew she was still at risk, but if we acted on the abuse she was being subjected to, it could make things even worse for her.

In the end all I could do was feed the information into the intelligence report about the gang leader she was involved with, but the whole experience convinced me that this was an area that needed detailed research and investigation with a better way to respond to situations such as these.

Shortly after the seminar, my work from the PRAS programme was published. The full report was called 'Missing You Already: A guide to the investigation of missing persons' and ran to 98 pages, accompanied by 'The Police Officers Guide to the Investigation of Missing Persons' and a tri-fold summary guide and pocket-sized cards containing key points to remember in the early stages of an investigation, also produced and distributed nationally across the force.

The prompts included things like:

Taking the initial report – be thorough and do not overlook the fact that this might be the initial report of a major crime
Family Liaison – make regular contact, give updates, ensure there is a point of contact for the family
Supervision – assess the level of risk, ongoing active supervision, consider a review by a CID supervisor after 48 hours

I was no longer shouting into a void. People were sitting up and taking notice of the concerns that weighed so heavily on me and others working in missing persons.

This was the result of countless hours of research in historic missing persons cases, methodically wading through hundreds of paper reports from dusty old boxes and talking to people who had been involved in such cases to identify gaps and failings in how the missing were dealt with. Reading it back in its final stages, I could clearly see how my more recent operational experiences had informed the report, due to there being far more information and data available than in many past cases. By extension, I knew that the experience of the many families whose loved ones had been let down by the existing processes also lived among its pages.

Although inroads were being made into improving the processes, some cases continued to remind me of the complexities that existed and how easy it was to try really hard and still miss something.

Nothing could bring Rob or the elderly man with dementia back, and I couldn't remove the pain from their families. But their experience had shone a light on this issue. In my acknowledgements, I made sure to highlight their importance in driving future change.

I should like to express my gratitude to those families, with whom I had personal contact, whose pain and suffering in coming to terms with a loved one going missing and sometimes not returning, was the catalyst for this research. Hopefully their suffering can in some way be mitigated if this work helps to improve procedures for the future.

There was a section dedicated to issues relating to those in care, looking broadly at the processes in place around those who went missing from children's homes, hospitals for residential care, facilities for the elderly and those who were physically and mentally disabled, where residents had greater vulnerabilities than the general population. My research had evidenced an issue that was widely recognised in the police, who received a high proportion of missing person reports from care establishments.

Many of the cases that I examined saw a significant proportion of reports coming from care staff stating that they could see a child in their care walking out of the grounds of the home and that they were going missing, or that the child had been told to be home by 10 p.m. and were missing because it was 10.15 p.m. and they were not back.

The question here was, were these really missing persons and was it the responsibility of the police to find them? Something that I would answer by asking what a reasonable parent would do in the same situation.

Guided by my experience with the young girls in Bletchley, and the knowledge I had developed from Juliet and Paul about trafficking, there was also a dedicated section on prostitution, broadening the definition from the stereotypical idea of 'tarts', 'pimps' and street vice, to a problem of sexual exploitation where vulnerable individuals were taken advantage of, not fully recognising what they have become involved in as prostitution.

I can now look back with hindsight and see that the case with the Bletchley girls was my first encounter with Child Sexual Exploitation (CSE). Some of the language used in the report now makes me uncomfortable. We used the phrase 'child prostitution' for example, a term which implies a level of consent and willingness. With the knowledge we have now, we know this cannot be the case and we would certainly never use such a term today.

At the time, we didn't have the same understanding of CSE as we do now. It was not something that was recognised or talked about. Although I later learned the missing girls were safely steered back into secure and normal lives, I now better understand my unease at the case's conclusion, and the sense that there was more that we should have done.

It would be several years before I encountered CSE again, in another part of the country. Only then was it even beginning to be properly recognised and investigated. The same was true with human trafficking. As I looked back over cases I worked or was familiar with, it was obvious that the indicators were all there. This type of exploitation had been occurring but was just not recognised.

We needed a standardised approach to missing persons nationally and a national reporting form, formal training in dealing specifically with missing person cases for police officers, and challenging the persistent attitude that mispers were a 'nuisance'.

It was also an issue that needed to be responded to correctly by all agencies and not something that I felt should always be the responsibility of the police, as with the children being late back to their care homes.

A similar situation also arose in hospitals. One particular case I came across saw a local hospital ring to report one of their patients missing from the Emergency Department, having walked out with a canula in their arm.

Several hours of police time was used to take the report and locate the person, only for them to be found at home. They had walked out of the hospital after becoming tired of waiting for treatment.

They were an adult patient and there was no medical risk from their leaving, so were they truly missing and was it really a police matter?

Cases like this fed the narrative that mispers were an inconvenience to police, which in turn led to a lack of attention to cases where people were genuinely missing.

Armed with the information in my report, I hoped that 'missing' would cease to be viewed as an isolated nuisance issue by police, and instead be seen as what I now knew it to be. An indicator – an indicator of something being wrong and potentially the first notification – of a murder, abduction or other serious offence.

So, for years now, my mantra has been that going missing is an indicator, telling everyone that I encountered that they should be trying to understand what was causing this behaviour. Even those who return safely had a reason for going missing in the first place.

In the twenty-two years since 'Missing You Already', as the report was published, I have continued to recognise the complexity of defining vulnerability and tried to encourage its expansion to beyond simple factors of age, physical and mental health. At the time I was pleased with the outcome and believed that it highlighted other, less obvious vulnerabilities that had often been missed up to that point. But I know now that we still had much more to learn. With every case I have worked or reviewed, and every element of research and guidance I have contributed to, these definitions have developed and broadened. Understanding vulnerability is vital in the field of missing persons and as the world and society changes with time it is always evolving – we must ensure we keep improving our responses to missing people.

It is a difficult and conflicting emotion to deal with, looking back in this way. So many unanswered questions remain around past cases and it's hard not to wonder what you could have done better. If you could have made more of a difference.

CHAPTER 6

Searching

Has the person's behaviour changed recently?

I woke with a start. It was the middle of the night and my phone was ringing. Bleary-eyed, I reached for the receiver.

Who could it be calling at this time? I wondered.

Good news rarely comes at this hour.

I had been seconded to the National Crime and Operations Faculty (NCOF) in 2003 to look at national guidance on missing persons.

It was another significant challenge, but I was ready for it. Whatever discomfort I felt about past decisions and responses to missing persons, I knew this was the way to take those lessons and turn them into something positive for the future.

'Hello?' I croaked, as I switched on a lamp and allowed my eyes to adjust to the light.

'Hi, Charlie, I am calling on behalf of ACC Page,' he said.

Mick Page had been promoted to assistant chief constable for Thames Valley Police since we had last worked together when I'd managed the operations department in Milton Keynes. Although our paths crossed from time to time, I was surprised to hear that he had asked for me to be contacted at this time of night.

'Hi,' I said. 'How can I help you at this hour?'

'Sorry for the late call, but we've got a big job going on down here, a missing person case, and we need you on it. Mr Page would like you to look at a search strategy,' he said. 'Can you get here as fast as you can?'

'What's the job?' I asked.

'It's quite a sensitive one and we really need some direction as to how to focus our activity,' he explained. 'You will get a full briefing when you get to the major incident room at Abingdon Police Station. We'd welcome the benefit of your thoughts.'

'Who's the missing person?' I asked, as I started to get ready.

'It's Dr David Kelly,' he said. 'The UN weapons inspector, works for the Ministry of Defence.'

I sucked in a sharp breath. This *was* going to be a sensitive one. I knew exactly who Dr Kelly was. In fact, most of the UK probably did. He was a biological weapons expert and distinguished government scientist whose extensive career had been dedicated to hunting down what had become known in the public consciousness as 'weapons of mass destruction'.

The government's dossier on Iraqi weapons of mass destruction had been published a year earlier in 2002 and contained a claim that some of Iraq's chemical and biological weapons could be deployed 'within forty-five minutes of an order to do so'.

Several months later, journalist Andrew Gilligan raised concerns over this claim in an explosive BBC Radio 4 *Today* broadcast on 29 May 2003, which led to accusations that the dossier had been 'sexed up' to legitimise the war in Iraq, based on information from a 'senior government official'.

The story set off a bitter row between the media and the government that had rumbled on for months. Just a week before Dr Kelly had been reported missing, he had been outed by the government as the 'senior government official' behind the story after it emerged that he'd had an unauthorised, off-the-record conversation with Andrew Gilligan about the dossier, sucking him into an enormous controversy.[2]

A few minutes after the call, I was in my car and driving along the near-deserted A-roads towards Abingdon Police Station. As I drove, I couldn't help but think how unusual a situation this was. I had been asked for strategic guidance on policy and its implementation around missing persons before, and I'd been called out to share my broader operational experience in the force. But being called out as a missing persons expert to assist on a live case wasn't something that happened regularly, and certainly not at this level.

Could it be that my current involvement in NCOF had prompted this invitation?

The project was going well and my only frustration was the bureaucracy around the position.

There was an embargo on secondments by some police forces, including Thames Valley, but it had been agreed that I could be released on a month-by-month basis to the faculty, which was based in Hampshire. While I was grateful to be allowed to participate, the process was deeply frustrating for two reasons. First, I had to reapply for the position every single month and wait for my application to be considered, which was a lot of paperwork that took me away from the tasks in hand. Second, I was never certain my reapplication would be approved, which left a

---

2   www.edition.cnn.com/2004/WORLD/europe/01/25/kelly. timeline/index.html

sense of uncertainty hanging over me. I hated leaving a job unfinished and was concerned what would happen if I didn't get the green light for the next month.

Despite my frustrations, this late-night call did seem to indicate the role had pushed me above the parapet and on to the front line of the missing. As ever, I was keen to make the most of the opportunity, but as I considered the case it felt quite daunting.

As the street lights flashed past, my head began to swim. I had to form an initial approach before I arrived. The information I had right now was scant, but that wasn't unusual at the start of a missing person case. While being aware of his high profile, what mattered were the circumstances of Dr Kelly's disappearance, so the first thing I would need to do on arrival was learn more about his state of mind, what he might have done, where he might have gone, and any leads that we already had.

The recent controversy he'd been embroiled in, in my mind at least, would likely have something to do with his going missing.

Missing was an indicator, after all.

But in all other ways, this was just like any other missing person case, and I had to treat it as such. We had to gather all the information we had, form a hypothesis, and then prove or disprove it.

When I pulled up to the police station forty-five minutes later, it was already a hive of activity. Station fully illuminated, there were dozens of cars parked up and people walking in and out of the building. It was proportional to the case, but certainly not normal for a station of its size and at that time of night.

I was pleased that I'd been called up to help, but as I locked my car and made my way to the station entrance, I suddenly felt under the spotlight. A flicker of doubt crossed my mind. I had become a missing person 'expert' almost by accident. Was I up to the job?

I took a deep breath and steeled myself. Now wasn't the time for self-doubt. Once again, I had said 'Yes I can help' to the opportunity in front of me. I'd just have to figure out exactly how I was going to do that as I went along.

I hope I get it right, I thought.

Thoughts flashed through my mind of other searches that I had been involved with. The murder investigation where I was part of the team sent out to find the offender who was living on a traveller site, but we did not know which one. We travelled all over the South-East of England, driving hundreds of miles, only to find him within two miles of our base. What about the missing person search where the officer in charge deployed helicopters, search teams, dogs and horses over a wide area, only to find that she was at a friend's house. Sometimes the resolution was right under your feet, but trying to justify a dramatic use of expensive resources was very tempting.

Remember, assess what we know and use the right resources to solve the problem.

As soon as I'd heard Dr Kelly's name, I knew this was going to be a critical incident for the force to get right, but the atmosphere in the incident room confirmed it. The place was vibrating with action and anxiety when I walked in.

As I entered the room, I could see it was heaving with police of various rank and expertise, including ACC Page, who was the senior officer present and in overall charge of the operation. The people who were present and the way that the station was set up spoke volumes about how seriously the incident was being taken – the presence of the ACC indicated to me that all eyes would be on us.

There were people nestled on banks of computers, logging information to make sure everything was properly recorded. Off the main room where all of the staff were based, there was also a press room and a separate office for the senior investigating officer. A host of police supervisors were also hovering around, anxious to keep things on track.

Given that national and even international media had been following the story relentlessly, Dr Kelly's disappearance would undoubtedly draw their attention. The allegations made against the government meant that the prime minister, Tony Blair, would also likely be watching how things unfolded.

It wasn't just me in the spotlight, it was all of us.

Across the room, I caught Mr Page's eye.

'Charlie, you're here,' he said, with a tense smile.

'I am,' I said, shaking his hand firmly. 'So, where are we up to?'

He gave me a rundown of all the established facts. Dr Kelly's family had stated that he was extremely distressed and anxious about the situation he was in. On the previous day, at 3 p.m., he had left his house wearing jeans, a white cotton shirt, a brown leather belt and brown shoes, telling his wife that he was going for a walk. But when he still hadn't returned by 11.45 p.m., his wife called the police and reported him missing. She'd stated that he had been gone for an unusually long time and his family was concerned for his welfare.

A helicopter had been sent up soon after, searching bridleways from Longworth to the River Thames, east to Newbridge and back to Kingston Bagpuize, near Abingdon, in case he was lost or had had an accident, but had found nothing.

There was a real urgency to get out there and do our best to find Dr Kelly, and after Mr Page's comprehensive briefing, he turned to me.

'So, what should we do, Charlie?' Mr Page asked.

I knew that I could lead this. Countless years of finding myself required to work things out on my own and find a way to the answer had taught me this. I was buoyed by the support of the assistant chief constable.

It didn't make the experience any less daunting though. I felt all eyes on me as I started to outline my approach, the resources we'd need and my decision as to how and where we should deploy search teams.

I reviewed all the information that I had been briefed on and talked to people in the incident room to check their accounts and their feelings about what had happened. I knew that I would have to consider other possibilities, and it might be appropriate to gather further information from the family later, but my immediate priority was working on the information that we had.

The family was being closely supported by a family liaison officer to ensure they were fully updated on the search, and to shield them from the media who we knew were likely to try to reach them. Information they had provided through officers revealed that a favourite local trail, up Harrowdown Hill, was a place that Dr Kelly would often walk.

I dug further into what was going on in Dr Kelly's life at the time, sifting through the information that had been gathered in the incident room since his disappearance. Four days earlier he had been questioned by the Foreign Affairs

Select Committee (FAC) about his conversations with Andrew Gilligan and the fact that he had been indicated as the main source of the *Today* story. He'd stated to the FAC that he did not believe he was the main source, but the BBC continued to refuse to discuss their source. The following day, Dr Kelly had also given evidence before the Intelligence and Security Committee (ISC), and all of this had been headline news.

It was clear this had been a time of immense stress for him, with his integrity being scrutinised and being placed as a key player in a scandal that could leave his reputation in tatters. I could only imagine what a weight it must have been to bear. What must it be like to be subject to so much public scrutiny? What about the impact on family, friends and professional contacts? Being unable to escape the spotlight of media attention? What would it mean for his future?

It didn't take me long to formulate what I believed to be the most likely hypothesis – suicide.

In cases such as these, it was essential to consider what was known from research and personal experience to build a hypothesis about what the missing person might have done and where they might go. Such trends and patterns were hugely useful, but care was needed in how they were interpreted and applied before any decision was made as to where to deploy resources.

The profile of people who attempted or completed suicide indicated that they would often go somewhere they could find peace, which had significance for them, or perhaps a picturesque view. Some would leave a suicide note and leave behind items such as keys and credit cards that would no longer be needed. Neither a note nor personal items were relevant in this situation, but the information about the local walk that the family had shared with us certainly was.

It was clear to me that Dr Kelly was extremely vulnerable and at risk. Under great pressure, I believed that he'd gone to this much-loved beauty spot to take his own life, because of the situation that he'd found himself in.

Of course, there *was* also a chance that we'd send a full search team crashing in, disturbing him as he tried to find some solitude and get his head straight. We had to always be open to other possibilities, but I felt the risk to him was sufficient for that possibility to be overridden.

The fact was that this person required an urgent and immediate response. He was at risk, and we couldn't just sit back and wait for full daylight to try and search for him. If my hypothesis was right, he might be sitting there right now, considering taking his life. If we acted now, perhaps he could be saved.

But this was the eternal search manager's dilemma. Decisions were always made in the knowledge that often there was no hard evidence to support what you were doing. It was all based on the most likely hypothesis. Deploying resources in the wrong place could mean the person was not found and could suffer further harm or die.

The pressure was immense, especially knowing that the decisions you made would be scrutinised based on the eventual outcome. Throwing every resource out there in the moment might make you look good at the time, but were they the right resources to find the person and how would it hold up when observers who had the benefit of 20/20 hindsight ripped your approach to pieces? That was always in your mind.

'*What are you doing? Is this right? Are you sure?*' These were the questions asked by your ACC, the media, even yourself. The truth was that you never knew for sure.

Then, on top of that, was the very personal thing that maybe this person's life was in your hands. That maybe the future for this person's family was in your hands. This was why it was so important to put all of that to one side and focus only on the facts: What do we know? What don't we know? What do we need to know? What are the resources we've got?

Based on that, my mind was set. Thoroughly searching Harrowdown Hill was our priority, to rule my idea in or out. Given my hypothesis that Dr Kelly was at high risk of suicide, I looked at the area and wanted to focus on the high spots of his usual route, particularly the top of Harrowdown Hill, and so deployed the search teams there.

There was always debate about searching for people in the dark, particularly on terrain that might be difficult, due to health and safety concerns. But police officers and search specialists were enlisted and paid, or volunteered, to do this job, and they got out there and did it when they were needed and instructed.

We had a defined search area, and the team was on its way, so I updated Mick on what I was doing. All I could do for the team then was listen over the radio and wait with bated breath for news or further information, offering strategic guidance where it was needed.

But there was no sitting around and twiddling thumbs. *Okay, what next?* I thought.

Remaining in the incident room, I was still responsible for setting the strategy, and that meant looking forward.

What if we didn't find him where we expected?
Where would we expand our parameters to?
What other resources might we need?

As well as going over the plan in action, I had to talk to others involved in the investigation who were following other lines of enquiry. It would take the search team about half an hour to get to Harrowdown Hill, but until they were there, we had to continue to keep our minds open to other possibilities. Had there been an accident? Is there somewhere else he might have gone? Was there any indication of foul play? It was essential to start planning for each of those eventualities as well.

Searching wasn't an exact science, nor was people's behaviour, so our priority was only ever our best plan based on the information we had, and patterns and trends drawn from behavioural assessments from past cases. Taking this overarching approach, rather than comparing to individual past cases, reduced the risk of being swayed by that individual's behaviour. Looking at what people *usually* did in a similar scenario gave you a far better starting point than putting all your eggs in one basket, and also a more rounded picture.

Of course, behaviour depended on so many different things, and there was always a chance that something else entirely had happened. But in this case, whichever angle I looked from, my gut told me that we were on the right track.

As the minutes ticked by, the tension thickened. We could hear the search teams inching closer to the brow of Harrowdown Hill, as they delivered regular updates over the radio.

Suddenly, the radio crackled to life again and the whole room leaned in to listen. It was a woman named Lou

Holmes, one of the civilian search volunteers and a dog handler with Bucks Search and Rescue.[3]

'I've found him,' she said. Then she paused. 'I think he's dead.'

Lou had been making her way along the search route when her dog, Brock, had started barking, indicating that he had found something. He was almost exactly where we had expected him to be, near the top of Harrowdown Hill, slumped with his back against a tree, looking out towards the view.

While the facts around the man's condition and identity were still to be established, most people knew a dead body when they saw one. The man also matched Dr Kelly's description, down to the clothes he had been wearing when he left his family home.

'Thank you,' I said. 'We'll get medics there to confirm and police to secure the scene. Can you share your exact location please?'

As she described her location, the pressure in the incident room began to slowly release and once again became a hive of activity, mobilising officers and medics to attend the scene, informing the family and arranging for the body to be identified, and working out how to manage the media when the news broke.

Nothing could take away the pain of the loss Dr Kelly's family would experience, but I was pleased we had found him. I was confident that we had done everything we could as properly and effectively as we could. We got a quick resolution, so it hadn't dragged on through the day.

---

3 www.bucksfreepress.co.uk/news/410092.search-and-rescue-dog-handler-tells-how-she-found-dr-kelly/

If that had happened, we'd have been swamped by media, the family would have been approached during a time of great upset, rumours would have circulated, and stories that we had no control over would have been published. It would have created a much worse ordeal for everyone involved.

I just hoped that our quick actions had saved the family from some of that distress and pain, although given the profile of the story around him, I knew that they would have a lot to face as they dealt with their loss and grief.

With the job done, I went outside to take in some fresh air and shake off the remnants of the tension of the incident room that still lingered. It appeared that Mick had the same idea.

'Mr Page,' I said, spotting him in the station's back yard. 'Thank you for asking me to assist with this. I appreciate you involving me.'

'We needed your insight, and you did a great job, thank you,' he said. 'By the way, how's the secondment going?'

'The role is great, but the process . . .' I said, rolling my eyes and shaking my head.

'What do you mean?' he asked. I couldn't hold back.

'It's an enormous pain. I have to reapply for it every single month,' I said, exasperated. 'That bloody Peter Neyroud and his secondments policy. It's important work; I don't see why I can't just get on with it!'

Mick stared at me, open-mouthed and said nothing. I looked back at him, slightly puzzled. I knew I wasn't one to usually launch into a tirade, but I'd thought Mick knew me well enough to understand. Then I felt a tap on my shoulder.

I turned round and my heart sank. There, standing behind me was Chief Constable Peter Neyroud. There was no wondering how long he'd been there – by the stern look on his face, I knew he had heard every word of my rant.

'Ah, good morning, sir,' I blustered. I wanted the ground to swallow me whole. *What had I done?*

We were probably only standing face to face for a couple of seconds, but it felt like an eternity as I imagined my whole career in missing going down the drain because I'd spoken out of line.

Well, Charlie, I thought, *you've done it now.*

I was about to break into a profuse apology when Peter's face cracked into a smile.

'OK, Charlie, you win. Have your secondment,' he said. 'Well done today.'

'Thank you, sir, and sorry about the rant,' I said, as he went on his way.

Safely out of earshot, I looked at Mick.

'Phew,' I said. 'That could have gone worse.'

'It could,' he said with a grin. 'But looks like you won't need to worry about reapplying for your secondment again.'

Shortly after Lou and Brock's discovery, the man was confirmed by medics to be deceased. There had been blood on his left side and his left wrist had been cut.

The media had been on to the development immediately and Thames Valley Police issued a statement saying that two separate investigations were under way – one into Dr Kelly's disappearance and another into the identity of a body that had been found.

It wasn't disingenuous. Until the body had been officially identified, both investigations had to remain open. I knew the chances were slim, but what if it wasn't Dr

Kelly? Where would we go next? What would be our next hypothesis?

Although I had to keep the possibility in mind, everything I knew and the inexplicable sense in my gut told me it was him.

Regardless of the fact the body hadn't been identified, almost immediately news stories started appearing online, with headlines like *Body matches Dr Kelly description*. It was frustrating but not unexpected, given the tragic conclusion of a story that had dominated the front pages for weeks.

The family identified Dr Kelly and the post-mortem took place the day after his body was found. In it, the coroner concluded that his cause of death was a haemorrhage caused by a self-inflicted injury from 'incised wounds to the left wrist', with the ingestion of co-proxamol painkiller tablets noted as a contributory factor.

The findings, for me, answered all the pertinent questions regarding what had happened to Dr Kelly, but the media and many members of the public felt differently. In the wake of the post-mortem, rumours and conspiracy theories began to circulate, suggesting elements of foul play, third party involvement and suggestions that Dr Kelly had been 'taken out'.

Despite the ongoing media furore, I took solace in the fact the case absolutely fitted a profile, and that was proven to be correct by what we had found. Because those two things fitted together, in my mind it didn't leave any room for the possibility of any other outcome. I just had to accept that there would always be people who speculated.

As my work continued, NCOF was subsumed into a new police body, the National Centre for Policing Excellence

(NCPE). Part of its focus was on developing national police guidance for all UK police forces and its first three focus subject areas were those that we were already working on, Domestic Violence, Child Abuse Investigation and Missing Persons, as they were considered the three highest risk areas of policing. A subject matter expert was put in charge of each area, and I continued to lead on missing persons, being tasked with creating specific guidance that could be used by forces across the country.

After six years of pushing the agenda so far, it was pleasing to see those at the top finally recognising the importance of missing.

However, working at such a senior level and creating guidance of this type was well outside my experience.

'Missing You Already' was a good starting point, but how should I develop it? How could I make it more relevant and accessible for other officers? How could I ensure that it was something useable, so the guidance was implemented, rather than just left gathering dust?

I had plenty of my own ideas, but I was just one person, and I didn't have the monopoly on good ideas.

Where would I have been in Rob's or the elderly man with dementia's case without Milton Keynes Search and Rescue? Or without children's services in the case of the young girls disappearing from Bletchley?

I wanted to engage police across the whole of the UK first, then other agencies and charities whose input I knew would be valuable. It was a significant task, so I created a process where each meeting I had helped inform the next. I organised regional meetings where I presented my ideas and asked for feedback, for attendees to share any experiences, ideas and approaches developed locally. After each meeting, I tweaked my ideas and presented the updated version at the next one. Working part-time at Bramshill and from home, with a considerable requirement for travel, I developed a model of working that was not nine to five and certainly not desk-based. I became something of a digital nomad, working on trains, in hotels, in cafes, in my car – anywhere that I found the space and clarity to work, and an opportunity to think outside the box.

At the same time, I identified other initiatives across the country, from police and other organisations, that were focused on missing persons, and I needed to visit them to get a broader sense of how we could improve going forward.

There was the development of a computerised missing persons management system in Gloucestershire Constabulary, and a scheme supporting the families of missing persons that was run by the National Missing Persons Helpline, for example. Research by The Children's Society titled 'Still Running' comprised interviews with children to find out why they had run away, which showed that the true number of runaways was way higher than the official figures showed. So many incredibly innovative projects for me to look into as I travelled extensively around the UK, soaking up all the knowledge like a sponge.

I found many other people who shared my passion for the missing and improving responses and approaches. In West Mercia, I found Phil Shakesheff who, like me, was focusing his energies on improving responses to missing people in his area; in West Yorkshire Alan Rhees-Cooper was working on solutions to the volume of misper reports the police received, and Deputy Assistant Commissioner Richard Bryan, who was chairing a national steering group on missing persons. All committed individuals, driven by the same purpose that I was.

I felt that one of the reasons my digitally nomadic approach to work was successful was because I was free of the interruptions and constraints of working in our offices in Bramshill. There was always someone arranging a meeting, asking for advice, or just generally milling around and that created distractions.

I knew in my gut that this piece of work was going to be vitally important. Having roamed the country gathering information, our team needed to decide what to include and turn it into a guidance document that police forces could actually use. We needed to be together and focused on our task, but the office wasn't going to be the right environment to get the best out of them.

It wasn't very orthodox, but I took advantage of the fact that we had been given complete autonomy over how we managed our work and rented a cottage in the countryside for a week.

It was just outside Watlington, in Oxfordshire, an hour away from the office and in a rural location, conveniently located near a quaint country pub, as I knew we would all need some rest and relaxation to get the job done.

The only rule I set was that we had a deadline to meet. By the end of the week, we had to have a completed version of the text, ready for submission.

Everyone seemed up for the challenge, and we all revelled in the naughtiness of doing something that wasn't the norm for a police project, but the focus of our goal remained.

For seven days, we wrote and rewrote drafts, talked through ideas, structure and how the document would be used practically. We cooked and ate together, discussed issues and how to resolve them, sometimes over a beer. We worked as and when we wanted, sometimes enjoying a lie-in and other times working late into the night, but definitely well over our usual hours, as was to be expected.

Whenever we hit a sticking point, we didn't just keep hammering away. We took a step back.

'I've had enough! Let's go for a walk,' someone would say, and off we would go.

As we walked, immersing ourselves in nature, listening to birdsong and talking about other things, our minds cleared. The conversation always naturally drifted back to the guidance. Refreshed and revived, the answers to the challenges would present themselves to us.

By the end of the week, we had achieved our objective and had a draft ready to go.

When we returned to the office, the other teams weren't quite in such fine fettle. They'd opted to take the more conventional route and work out of the office. They looked stressed, exhausted and were still working on their documents – exactly what I hadn't wanted for my own team.

There was no doubt that it had been hard work delivered under immense pressure, but along with a complete document titled 'Association of Chief Police Officers (ACPO) Guidance on the Management, Recording and Investigation of Missing Persons', we all emerged from the project invigorated and beaming with satisfaction and pride.

As we waited for the publication of the guidance, I was lucky enough to experience another considerable moment of pride, when I – along with others involved – were awarded a Thames Valley Police commendation for my work in the Dr Kelly case.

'Sergeant Charles Hedges is commended for his invaluable advice and guidance in respect of establishing search criteria during the initial stages of the inquiry, which was a major contributory factor to the early discovery of Dr Kelly's body.'

Although not my first commendation, this one held significant meaning for me. Although I was now considered a go-to person in the field of the missing for the police, this was my first formal recognition among my peers.

At the time of the case, I had done my usual 'Say yes, work out how later' and stepped up to the challenge. As I'd stuck my head above the parapet, I'd had to hope that I didn't get shot, like I had done in Rob's case, when I found myself under investigation.

This had rumbled on in the background for a few years but had come to a positive conclusion some time earlier. I had received a letter from the director of The Police Complaints Authority, who wrote to me telling me that no blame was attached to my actions and that in fact I was the person who got things right.

It felt good to be exonerated, but what was even more important to me was that, since that case – where mistakes had clearly been made nonetheless – I'd taken steps to make changes in how missing persons were dealt with, to prevent any family going through what Rob's had. I had seen the issues and made it my mission to address them.

As the guidance was published, I was already working on another publication in my role as a 'Doctrine Developer'. The title of my role was influenced by the head of the NCPE Sir David Phillips, a former chief constable who saw police guidance as akin to military doctrine.

Military doctrine was the expression of how military forces contributed to campaigns, major operations, battles and engagements; a guide to action, rather than a set of rules, that provided a common frame of reference across the military. Our guidance documents were intended to be the same for the police service, themed manuals to improve service and response and ensure that we were all singing from the same hymn sheet.

I had been asked to work on an ACPO project to deliver just that, a complete search manual.

While working on the project, I was fortunate enough to secure a former chief inspector, Clive Sims, as a secondee, assigning him just after he had retired from the police. I had met Clive when he was a senior search trainer at the Police National Search Centre, an experienced search practitioner and a Police Search Advisor (PolSA).

PolSAs were the search experts of the police service. They had their origins in counter-terrorism, following the 1984 Brighton bombing when the Provisional IRA had planted a bomb in the city's Grand Hotel, timed to explode while the Conservative Party Conference was taking place. The bomb detonated and five people were killed and 31 injured. The shocking event exposed a need for police to be trained in search and explosive devices, which had previously only been a military specialism.

Their techniques needed to be properly documented so they were available to all officers across the UK police forces.

Having Clive on board was a real coup for the project. He was renowned for telling senior officers responsible for planning and managing operations, 'Don't let your mismanagement become my emergency,' an example of his invaluable wit and wisdom that would inform the guidance!

We were also ably assisted by another friend and colleague, Mark Harrison, who was the National Search

Advisor at the NCPE. Many years before, Mark and I had been sergeants in our respective forces, and he would sometimes visit me in my office where we would discuss what we dreamt of doing in the coming years. We both exceeded our imaginings as to how we would progress.

As well as documenting the techniques used by PolSAs, we also needed to integrate those used by other agencies and specialist services and advise on how to work with them. Although in most cases, police had primacy in search, there were times when these other bodies had expertise which exceeded that of the police, such as marine and mountain rescue.

This was something I'd learned first-hand in September 1999, when training as a search manager under the Mountain Rescue Council (MRC) at Bangor University, which had been a truly eye-opening experience.

The course had endowed me with specific knowledge about how to plan and manage a search based on established and tried-and-tested methods. I had been self-taught up to that point and had made my own way both with Rob and the gentleman with dementia's cases, leaning on the expertise of my colleagues in local search and rescue services and departments.

By the time I had been asked to support the Dr Kelly case, I had the MRC's knowledge in my toolkit, and applied it to ensure he was found swiftly. The crux of it was assessing the information and deciding what could be done quickly, known as a 'hasty search'. This involved getting out there to cover the most likely areas in the hope of finding the person, while simultaneously taking the time to plan a more detailed search, just as we had done.

The classroom-based course also covered topics such as what resources should be used, and how they should be briefed, deployed and managed. It emphasised the importance of feedback at the end of each search segment, determining probability of detection, ascertaining which areas should be searched again, and the use of overlapping searches to improve the chances of finding someone by searching an area more than once but using different 'search assets', like people on foot, dogs and aerial resources like helicopters and drones.

The development of technology had enhanced the ability to search more quickly and thoroughly, with assets like drones having the potential to provide quicker and easier access to difficult terrain. Technology that tracked the location of searchers was also enabling accurate mapping of the areas that they had covered and – more importantly – those that had not been covered. It was all very innovative, and the potential was extremely exciting, but as well as knowing what was available, skill was required in knowing what to deploy in which circumstances, and how to do so in the most effective manner.

My office moved to Wyboston in Bedfordshire, where Clive and I looked at specialist techniques for searching cars, houses, commercial vehicles, aeroplanes, boats, open spaces, water, forests and mountains, among many other locations and terrains.

Every different search location had different considerations. Searching a vehicle, vessel, or even aircraft, for example, you had to understand their construction, so you knew where there were spaces for people or items to hide or be hidden, as well as know how they had been used in the past in similar scenarios.

Without that knowledge, how would searchers know that there was enough space behind the dashboard of a car to hide a person? This was a tactic that has been employed by people smugglers, but without that specialist search knowledge, you would not believe there was a big enough void there.

Each type of terrain also tested searchers in distinct ways, with water being one of the most challenging. In most cases, visibility was extremely poor, with divers having to rely on feeling for objects with their hands. This limited the size of the area they could search and could also make for an unpleasant experience when encountering a body, which might sink or float depending on changes as the amount of time spent in the water passes.

The movement of objects underwater were also complicated by currents and tides, and there was no exact science for the movement of bodies in water, with the many experts I had spoken to on the matter having very different opinions from one another and in each situation.

As I continued to explore the intricacies of searching for people and objects in both man-made and natural terrains, I maintained my personal habit of turning to nature and taking to the outdoors to sustain my work-life balance. With another long-time friend and walking companion, Mark, we decided to undertake the National Three Peaks Challenge, climbing the three highest peaks in Scotland, England and Wales – Ben Nevis, Scafell Pike and Snowdon respectively – in twenty-four hours.

While a great opportunity to gain clarity and perspective, the challenge also had many overlaps with my ongoing work project, not least in understanding the challenges and dangers of search.

Having never tackled Ben Nevis before, we decided to go to Scotland four weeks before the challenge, to climb it and understand the terrain. The weather wasn't great, though not bad enough for us to call off the training climb.

Despite encountering heavy snow at the summit, we seemed to have completed the climb without too much issue. Or so I believed, but as we started our descent in the still-falling snow, I realised in horror that as we had ascended, we had come dangerously close to a cornice – an overhanging ledge of snow high above the valley floor – without even realising.

If we'd walked on it, it might have broken away beneath our feet, with potentially fatal consequences.

I was horrified. As a search manager, I should have known better.

It was a stark reminder of the hazards of walking in bad weather conditions and the importance of the skills required for safe and effective search techniques.

It certainly helped focus our minds as the day of the challenge approached, and we made sure we had everything in place. The challenge included driving between each mountain, 462 miles in total, so we recruited the help of my then partner Shelley and her best friend Kerrie as our driving team.

Shelley and I had started out as neighbours years earlier. We'd become close friends, and she was a great support when my long and irregular work hours had made it difficult for me to always get home to attend to my elderly mother, who was in a nursing home, then in hospital, shortly before she died. When I was in need of support, Shelley would breeze in with a simple, 'I'll pop by and see her, Charlie.'

We'd seen one another rebuilding our lives after both of our marriages broke down, and that friendship had grown and evolved over time, eventually blossoming into a relationship.

Shelley and Kerrie stayed with our vehicle, as Mark and I enjoyed a straightforward climb and descent at Nevis. But by the time we reached Scafell Pike we were tired from one hard climb and running on very little sleep.

It was the middle of the night and very dark as we started the hard slog up, but with the path ahead illuminated by the head torches of others who were undertaking the challenge. As we headed up the track, I could hear Shelley in the distance.

'I love you, Charlie Hedges,' she shouted, echoing around the hills.

I smiled to myself. It was always good to know that we cared for each other, and she supported my ambitions and vision. I'd learned much about that in my professional and personal life, and the support drove me on. I wasn't quite sure how I'd do any of it without her.

With Scafell eventually conquered, we made the long journey on the M6 to Snowdon. All four of us tackled this final ascent and our efforts were richly rewarded by a clear day, and at the summit the sun shone across the magnificent views of the surrounding countryside; despite having climbed Snowdon on several previous occasions, this was the first time that I had good visibility and could enjoy the views.

We completed the descent from Snowdon with just a few minutes to spare in our 24-hour window, exhausted and exhilarated in equal measure. A break in nature once again gave me some much-needed clarity and calm and I returned to work refreshed, clear-headed and ready to take on my next challenge.

Back at the office, I fed all my prior knowledge, plus learnings from my recent personal experience, into the manual, alongside information from my team's experience, and the conversations and consultations Clive and I had held with customs officers, coastguards, mountain and lowland rescue and underwater search teams.

Each search specialist had unique expertise and extremely specific knowledge, and it was vital to gather all of that information.

The customs officers who knew all the tricks and techniques for smuggling items and even people across borders; the coastguards who were intimately familiar with the hazards and risks when searching the shore and sea; and land and mountain search experts who understood how the direction of the wind would affect the outcome of a dog search – their knowledge could all be used to enhance basic search techniques to make them as effective as possible.

We had a remit to write about any aspect of search that was relevant to the police, and we made sure we covered them all off.

What resulted was a guide, published in 2006 with the title, 'Practice Advice on Search Management and Procedures', that compiled information on search planning and management, incorporating the best search techniques available and a specific segment on searching for missing people – a doctrine on search for the entire UK force.

Throughout my career, my work has required a wide range of skills to be able to conduct or oversee investigations and searches. Search is a particularly challenging part of finding missing persons and both developing the search guidance in 2006 and working with Clive improved my knowledge greatly.

After I qualified as a search manager, I called Roger from Milton Keynes Search and Rescue, who had urged me to go on the course, to let him know. His response was: 'Welcome to the legion of the damned.' To this day it remains one of the best descriptions I have ever heard, given the complexities and uncertainties of search and in decision-making. The truth is, you can be damned if you do, and damned if you don't follow a particular search strategy.

The UK Police National Search Centre defined search as 'The capability to locate specified targets using intelligence assessments, systematic procedures and appropriate detection techniques.' Confusingly, in many other countries, search has a much more general application, with the search for a missing person encompassing all activities to locate them, including what police in the UK would think of as investigation.

In the guidance documents I wrote, I talked about a circle of activity that never ends until a missing person is found – investigate, search and review. The investigation finds information that leads to further investigation or informs the need for search; search looks for clues or evidence; everything is under constant review and leads back to further investigation and search activity, until such a point when the missing person is located.

The guidance also relates to 'scenario-based' or 'hypothesis-based' searching – the terms are interchangeable in police parlance. This means looking at the information that is available and considering what the most likely explanations are for what has happened based on experience, research and/or behavioural data.

The more that is known about the missing person the better, and it may be necessary to ask some difficult questions to establish what sort of person they are and what has been happening in their life, known in policing circles as 'victimology', as I discovered in the case of Dr David Kelly. It was only by understanding his state of mind and identifying his suicide risk that we could explore that particular profile.

The guidance also referred to Grampian Police research, undertaken by my long-time friend Graham Gibb, whom I met on the PRAS programme and with whom I remained in close contact due to our shared passion for missing issues, and Dr Penny Woolnough. The research was based on a study of over 3,000 missing person cases in the UK and provided useful insights into missing person behaviour that could be used to develop search strategies.

The research showed that people who take their own life generally do not travel a great distance on foot to do so, as they have decided on the course of action and just want to carry it out – as was demonstrated in Dr Kelly's case. It also highlighted that they might travel a long way by car to get to their intended place to carry out the act of suicide, but they kill themselves relatively close to their car – 80 per cent within 500–600 metres of their vehicle.

The research also highlighted some simple clues, such as when teenagers go missing, girls tend to be at friends' houses, while boys tend to be on the streets. At the time, Grampian's data showed that in missing children between the ages of 5 and 8 years old, 70 per cent were found within 1.1 kilometres of the place they went missing.

When under pressure to find a missing child, there is a tendency to throw everything at it, which is correct but needs to be done in a focused manner, and the clues that data and research highlight can help set priorities, and reinforce things that might seem obvious, but signpost to where the focus of a search should be.

A more recent case where we have seen the importance and indeed challenges of search is the case of Nicola Bulley, a woman from St Michael's on Wyre in Lancashire who went for a walk with her dog while listening to a work meeting on her phone, before disappearing within a ten-minute time frame. Her dog, dog harness and mobile phone were all found on or near a bench close to the river Wyre.

From the outset, the police stated that their main hypothesis was that she had fallen in the water. It was a hypothesis that I totally agreed with. Based on twenty-six years' experience of missing persons and search, it was always the most likely thing to have happened.

But there were still questions and other possibilities that Lancashire Constabulary had to consider. If she did go in the water, was it an accident or was there another person involved? Was there something happening in her life that would make her want to disappear?

The case attracted an incredible amount of attention, with members of the public playing armchair detective and speculating online and in the media. The force revealed personal details about Nicola's life – the circumstances that are so important when investigating such cases.

These factors most likely informed other hypotheses the force was considering as they worked through that circular process of investigation, search and review, with drowning remaining the primary hypothesis until proven otherwise. Releasing this information caused a huge stir in the media and much adverse comment, although a subsequent review by the Information Commissioner's Office did not lead to any enforcement action.

Even when Nicola's body was eventually found by a couple walking in the area, twenty-three days after she had gone missing and about a mile downstream from St Michael's on Wyre, the speculation did not end. There were suggestions of suicide and even cries of foul play and cover-up, with people suggesting that Nicola may have been killed and then later dumped in the water, to make it appear in line with police hypothesis.

However, an inquest in June 2023 found Nicola's cause of death to be accidental drowning, with experts telling the hearing that entering cold water could cause a person to gasp and inhale water and drown in seconds. The first and most likely hypothesis that had been established was found to be true.

When a search begins, there is naturally much speculation and guesswork. There are so many gaps in knowledge at the start and, even as you fill them, it is a constantly moving picture, because unlike missing objects, missing people often move – either of their own volition or carried because of the terrain in which they have found themselves.

The approach to search is much more structured and professional than it was in my early days of policing, in fact much has changed in the discipline over the years, with improved techniques, training and access to resources.

Approaches and resources that were once seen as fanciful are now effective mainstays. I remember Sir David Phillips from the NCPE used to talk about the benefits of using drones in policing when they were hardly known about. He was derided at the time, but he was right, and they are now widely used in police searches today. But it is important to remember that search is not an exact science; it is a complex, challenging and ever-changing art, which we have to do our best to keep pace with.

CHAPTER 7

Exploited

Consider if they might be the victim of sexual exploitation

After thirty years' service in the police, it was time to retire, so in February 2007 I handed in my notice and left. Except, I didn't really leave. Being the person that left the police one day and started work again the next day was something I swore I would never do. But I was involved in something that I believed to be important, and I was finding very enjoyable and fulfilling. So, the day after retiring, I continued in my role as a 'Doctrine Developer' at the NCPE, only in a civilian capacity.

My policing years behind me, I looked forward to the new challenges that lay ahead in my civilian role, and the potential to focus even more on dealing with the missing. My gruff northern senior officer, however, seemed to have different ideas.

'If you think you are going to continue to work on missing from home, think on,' he told me, indicating that I would be directed to projects in other areas.

In a way, he was right. As a change in government policy saw the NCPE closed and transformed into the newly formed National Policing Improvement Agency (NPIA), I found myself once again under the leadership of my former chief constable, Peter Neyroud. My next two guidance projects focused on Stop and Search and Stop and Search in relation to terrorism, which were to be my last new guidance documents.

They were two hugely challenging and contentious subjects with political sensitivities that gave me a wealth of valuable insights into racism and bias. While I relished the tasks, I was always drawn back to the missing. In everything I did, I could see overlaps and opportunities for improvement, and I guess that when I thought circumstances warranted it, I was not very good at following orders. I could not pull myself away from the issue of the mission and set my sights on a new goal at the national Missing Persons Bureau.

As with many national functions, the Missing Persons Bureau was located at New Scotland Yard under the Met Police, but even the inspector in charge of it, Ravi Pillai, was dissatisfied with its functions and the constraints placed around the way it operated. We both shared a vision for the bureau as a national policing unit within the NPIA and away from the Met, so it could be better funded and resourced and have a role that served the needs of missing people and the police service across the UK.

We shared our ideas with anyone relevant whom we could persuade to listen, and they began to gain traction. A review of the service was launched and its outcomes supported our suggestions. As bids were invited for the creation of this newly created bureau, I set my sights on making myself its manager, with a vision to make it an operationally focused unit, advising and supporting police forces with the most difficult cases and bringing together the best practices that existed.

Although my big plan was torpedoed by a bid from the Serious Crime Analysis Unit (SCAS), which was appointed to take over the bureau, along the way and under the leadership of Joe Apps, I managed to land what turned out to be my dream job, as its national liaison officer, with carte blanche to create the role as I saw fit.

The Bureau didn't offer the level of operational support that I had envisioned, but it established itself as a nationally recognised unit that linked all missing person activity. For my part, I roamed the country, using the contacts I had made developing missing persons guidance to bring together all police forces, charities and other agencies into one cohesive network, identifying and sharing good practice and giving the operational support that I believed to be essential.

On my travels, I connected with a charity in Derby called Safe and Sound, whose focus was on exploited children. The organisation's founder and my main contact was Sheila Taylor, who saw me as a good listener and sounding board at a national level.

She told me many stories of the dreadful harm that children, some as young as seven or eight, were suffering at the hands of exploitative men, although we later learned that sometimes women were exploiters as well.

'They're coming to us with sexually transmitted infections as a result of rape and abuse,' she told me. 'It's truly horrific.'

Our conversations continued over the course of several months and a real sense of trust was built between us. We shared many of the same concerns and each story that Sheila shared with me from the front line of the charity's work was, to me, a clear indication: the instances they were seeing of children going missing could be a sign of exploitation.

I had no idea what the scale of the problem was though, until, one day, Sheila made her opening gambit.

'You know, Charlie,' she said. 'We have potentially a hundred victims and up to twenty suspects just in our area, and we want the police to deal with it. How do we get it across the line?'

The charity had amassed significant information about the victims and alleged offenders over several months. Many of the victims were repeatedly going missing. Looking at the movement of the suspects, whenever there was a possibility that they had drawn the interest of the authorities, it was clear that they were swapping areas, with others doing the same in other towns and cities.

Sheila and I both believed that we were dealing with organised crime groups, something that was not recognised by others in policing. They said that each incident was 'just happening'. But like Sheila, I saw it differently. There were clear patterns. The same names, locations, vehicles and timings cropping up again and again.

It was just like in the Bletchley case.

What had been an inkling for me then, due to the limited understanding or acceptance of child sex exploitation (CSE) in the police, suddenly appeared as plain as day. I shuddered at the thought of what I might have been dealing with at the time, and the abuse those girls may have been subjected to sickened me.

I completely believed the concerns held by the charity were valid, but I was shocked to learn how little progress had been made in the area. I had been party to conversations that had been opened about CSE and human trafficking years earlier, yet police and other organisations were still dismissing Sheila's concerns, despite what I viewed as clear indications of risk.

I could see the same attitude as there had been at the outset when the girls in Bletchley started going missing

– each case viewed in isolation, with no one in the police joining the dots.

But Sheila was. As she explained exactly what the team at Safe and Sound knew, she turned to me.

'I know we have a major problem here, and it needs to be dealt with,' she said. 'Can you help us?'

One of the major problems Sheila and her team were facing was the fact that the police couldn't accept the information they were gathering. There were strict protocols and requirements for collecting information in the police, which relied heavily on being able to verify the source and what they were telling you, all supported by a clear and detailed series of records.

What the charity was receiving were snippets of information, some from the girls themselves as they built trust with them, some from children's services, and they were trying to pull them together. But the data was not being recorded in a way that fitted police standards, simply because the team did not know what they were.

For the police to act on the charity's information, Safe and Sound needed to improve their collecting and recording of the information, and there also needed to be a shift in recognition of the problem.

While the former was a manageable but significant challenge in terms of administrative labour, the latter was something of an uphill battle. It was only a change of leadership that provided us with some welcome traction. Detective Superintendent Debbie Platt was a new arrival in child protection at Derbyshire Police, and she took great interest in the work that Safe and Sound were undertaking.

Debbie brought fresh eyes and a new perspective to the situation and seemed to really grasp the risk that Sheila was highlighting. She was determined to act, even if her decisions might be unpopular with her colleagues, due to the significant demand it would place on already-stretched resources.

Debbie and Sheila worked closely together on transforming the charity's data into something that could be accepted, and I provided guidance and support to Sheila using my insight and experience from working in the police service.

A robust information-gathering process was put in place and the charity's existing information analysed and converted into something useable, leading to the first steps of an investigation.

The charity was one step closer to being able to pursue its case.

Data wasn't the only challenge. Just as in the Bletchley case, not all of the victims were willing to talk about what was happening to them. Sheila's team were working hard to try to persuade them, but it wasn't easy.

Many people found it hard to engage with the police through distrust or fear of officialdom, and the victims in this situation were no exception. As a third sector organisation, Safe and Sound were having more success encouraging many of the girls to share their experiences.

As I'd seen in Bletchley, a key issue with the police was resources. When the girls had been going missing and turning back up, there had been attempts to follow up through 'safe and well checks', but this was a task undertaken by police officers who might not have had any contact with the girls before. They'd drop in, ask them what had happened, then the radio would crackle and they'd be called to the next job. There was no time to build trust and get other information out. If the girls shared nothing, that would be the end of it, until they disappeared again.

Safe and Sound had more time and resources to dedicate to sending the same people, providing opportunities to build relationships with the girls, but progress was still slow. The key difficulty was that the girls were being groomed by their perpetrators and told to say nothing and distrust anyone in a position of authority.

It became clear to us that the suspects were not only organised, but master manipulators. All the victims were vulnerable in one way or another, or even multiple ways, and these men identified these vulnerabilities and used them to keep them under their control. We repeatedly saw the same ruses, persuading them that what was happening was normal; bribing them with gifts and treats and saying that their parents were not concerned, they were just not allowing them to be themselves.

We were also seeing signs of the 'lover-boy' model being used among the victims. This tactic saw a young girl approached by a slightly older boy, someone whom the girl might see as a potential boyfriend. They would shower the girl with attention, make her feel special by picking her up and driving her around in his car, and treat her like a 'grown-up' by giving her cigarettes, alcohol and other inducements.

One such case that came to our attention was of a fourteen-year-old girl who was befriended by an older boy. He was in his late teens and had a rather smart-looking sporty car, in which he would turn up at the girl's school, initially giving her lifts home, but later taking her to other places. He plied her with gifts, introduced her to alcohol and cigarettes, and took her to parties that were filled with other older boys and girls. Of course, this made the girl feel special and grown up. It was something she could show off to her friends about.

This was almost textbook in the 'lover-boy' model. Like other young girls who had been targeted, she might have found herself feeling as though the pair had fallen in love, or at least that they had built a trust bond. This was the point when the 'lover boy' would have his victim where he wanted her – under his control. This was also when terrible things would start to happen.

After seducing our victim, the 'lover boy' in our case had introduced her to his male friends. He'd made it clear he wanted her to be friendly with them, and she had explained how he hadn't been cross when they started to touch her inappropriately, even though she was uncomfortable.

This behaviour escalated and before long, the abuse started. She was passed on to an older male, a gang leader for whom the 'lover boy' had merely been a pawn. Through power and fear she was forced into having sex with many other men, an object for them to use and share around.

Like other victims entrapped using this model, she might have felt like she couldn't decline these demands because of the previous 'kindness' shown to her through the gifts and lifestyle provided, or because she had been brainwashed to believe this was what an 'adult' relationship looked like.

Her 'lover boy' had convinced her that parents or other adults were out of touch with the 'real world' and didn't understand young people's lives, so listening to them was stupid and confiding in them was pointless. He also threatened to leave her and played on the naivety and insecurity that was natural for her age, by asking what her friends would think of her if she lost her grown-up boyfriend.

Often, though, they would simply be scared. Our victim was in too deep to talk to her parents and had been convinced that the police and other officials would be out to get her if she told them what was happening. She was trapped.

Once the victim was under this level of control, the suspect no longer needed to hide behind a façade of care or love, and instead would use violence or threats of violence to ensure they remained compliant. This made it very difficult for victims to speak about their experiences. Although they were being subjected to horrific violence, rape and abuse, they were still terrified of the repercussions of telling someone what was happening, for fear that it could get much worse.

Part of the brainwashing in such situations was to undermine any trust of those in authority or supportive organisations, and Sheila's team had a tough job of getting the girls to engage with them. I could understand their perspective. They either still trusted the 'lover boy' or, having been lured into what they thought was a friendship or relationship, they'd found their trust broken by their abusers.

To the uninitiated, this looked like difficult or unco-operative behaviour by the victim to the police and other organisations, all too often leading to them not getting help or support.

But why would they trust anyone else?

The team persisted regardless, and even the smallest wins were celebrated. One day, attending a meeting with Sheila at the Safe and Sound offices, the door suddenly burst open and one of their support workers flew into the room. Clearly something momentous had happened and we were all eager to hear what it was. She hovered by the door, clearly aware that maybe she should not have burst into the room, but unable to stop herself, eyes shining and unable to contain her excitement.

She explained that she had been visiting one of their victims at home for about nine months but had never got further than the outside of the house. Every time she turned up, the girl would shout at her from an upstairs window, spit at her and tell her to fuck off, before slamming the window closed.

She'd lost count of the number of visits she'd made, but finally, today had been different.

'I saw her at the window and expected the usual,' she said. 'But this time, she just looked down and said, "Oh, it's you," no spitting or swearing, just closed the window quietly.'

'That's great; thank you for persevering and caring,' Sheila said.

The girl wasn't part of the CSE investigation, but she was a victim in similar circumstances. This interaction reinforced what I was learning: just how difficult this type of case was to deal with.

I was stunned by the level of commitment and patience that was being shown. Trust was building, even if it was slowly. It was a huge breakthrough made possible by the care worker's patience and perseverance, which later led to further breakthroughs. The girl eventually opened up, allowed the charity to help and was happily steered back to a safe and successful life.

As the Safe and Sound team on the ground worked tirelessly to engage victims in building the case, Sheila, Debbie and I persevered with the wider investigation. I was using my national position and network of police contacts to muster support for what Debbie was trying to achieve – acceptance that organised crime groups were operating in the area.

Despite the idea still being dismissed by many, Debbie stood firm.

Away from that wider mission, the turning point in the investigation came when two police officers in Staffordshire did a routine vehicle check, concerned when they saw three men with two young girls in their car.[4] They had thought something was amiss and they'd been right.

The two girls had previously been reported missing from a care home in Derby. The men were arrested and later released without charge, but they were kept under surveillance and Derbyshire Police were alerted. A referral was made to the newly created sexual exploitation unit at Derbyshire Police. From this, Operation Retriever was commenced with the purpose of investigating what was going on.

I was in regular contact with Safe and Sound and Derbyshire Police, wanting to do anything I could to support such an important and groundbreaking investigation. Nothing like it had been done before and not everyone was convinced that what we were saying was actually happening. But a conversation with Sheila only served to support our concerns about the severity of the issue.

'When I left here last night, there was a man hanging around outside,' Sheila said. 'He followed me as I walked down the street to where my car was parked.'

'Did anything happen?' I asked, concerned for Sheila's safety.

---

4   www.bbc.co.uk/news/uk-11819732

'No, but the way he looked at me as he followed me, I am sure he was trying to intimidate me,' she said.

Clearly, we were making an impact, but unfortunately more direct action was not yet on the agenda. We discussed safety measures that Sheila and her team should take as the investigation progressed and hoped that there would not be any further incidents.

The key suspects were eventually identified as Abid Saddique and Mohammed Liaqat. At the time of the vehicle stop by Staffordshire Police, it emerged that Saddique was wearing an electronic tag, having been convicted of an assault on a woman.

Even with the green light, increased information on the suspects and some engagement from victims, it wasn't plain sailing. It quickly became clear that normal investigative methods would not work. Some of the victims, through careful and consistent engagement with Safe and Sound, had shared snippets of information that were enough to give direction to the police work, but it was not enough to provide the hard evidence needed to make arrests.

'There's only one way to get insight into what's really happening,' Debbie said one day. 'Covert surveillance.'

Covert surveillance was surveillance undertaken in such a manner that ensures the subject is unaware that it is or may be taking place. It was an extremely valuable investigative technique and regularly used in cases that warranted it, a tried and tested police method of gathering evidence. But for Operation Retriever, it wasn't straightforward. The victims would be seen, potentially meeting people, and going to addresses that were believed to be the sources of the abuse. I understood the challenge immediately.

'So, that means the police could be watching child victims walk into potentially abusive situations,' I clarified.

'Yes,' Debbie said. 'It's going to be difficult, but I believe it's the only way we can stop this.'

I was inclined to agree with her, and I respected her bravery in taking such a controversial approach. The decision had to be made quickly as we knew that girls were at risk and being exploited, but it was essential that all risks associated with using surveillance were assessed and mitigating factors employed. A number of difficult and soul-searching meetings passed, during which time Debbie and her plan drew lots of criticism from those outside the heart of this extremely difficult case.

In the end, a decision was made to undertake the complicated and highly controversial covert surveillance. Everyone inside Operation Retriever knew that without evidence that would stand up in court, nothing would be done to tackle this horrendous activity. The men responsible would evade justice, the current victims would continue to be abused and new victims would continue to be recruited.

The risks were high but, without taking them, how else was the abuse to be stopped?

The planning was meticulous, and it was agreed that the surveillance was to go ahead with a child protection professional deployed alongside the surveillance teams, to carefully monitor the risks and dictate when action should be taken to protect the child, even if it meant compromising the surveillance.

As the investigation began in earnest, the men's silver BMW was tailed by police and footage was gathered showing them cruising around Derby after midnight, apparently looking for vulnerable young girls. When they spotted a young pair at the side of the road, they stopped and tried repeatedly to entice the girls to get into the car.

Officers and a safeguarding professional were monitoring the situation in cars and on foot, following the suspects, identifying key addresses and witnessing their actions. They were there and always ready to stop surveillance and step in, should either of the girls enter the car, but neither did. In a later stop of the vehicle, police found bottles of vodka and plastic cups hidden under the seats so the underage victims could be plied with drink.

As more locations and suspects were monitored, another element began to raise comment around the profiles of the suspects. It emerged that the majority came from non-white backgrounds. As I supported the investigation team, I recalled that during my early days of policing, there were regular comments about Asian taxi drivers who were seen to be frequenting the vicinity's children's care homes, from which the children would often go missing.

Many of these passing observations hadn't been considered pertinent enough to warrant further investigation, but then taken in isolation, why would they? I knew that back then no one was connecting the dots, looking at the full picture – so, what might have been missed because of that?

The surveillance on Saddique, Liaqat and others involved continued until 24 April 2009, when police were watching a flat in Derby that had come to their attention during the investigation. Two distressed teenagers had emerged tearfully from the flat and called 999.

Unaware that they had been inside the building, the police responded immediately and took the girls to safety. The girls said that they had been raped, and made allegations against Saddique and Liaqat.

As they talked, they reeled off the names of other girls who had been abused.

A pattern emerged. Each victim led to more victims and more suspects. The full, horrific picture began to emerge. As we watched this unfold, I discussed developments with Sheila.

'Well, you were right, your concerns were correct and now we are seeing the full extent of what is happening,' I said.

'Nobody really believed that what we were talking about was happening,' Sheila replied. 'Now they are shocked by the extent and numbers of victims involved.'

I think that for all of us who were involved with this investigation we knew that it was big, but the scale and nature of the abuse and exploitation was far worse than we could have imagined.

Most of the girls were aged between twelve and eighteen, vulnerable and from troubled backgrounds, with some even younger. Many regularly went missing and some were in care homes or known to social services. Like in the 'loverboy' approach, they'd been targeted on estates or when walking home from school and befriended by the men, who invited them out for a drive or supplied them with alcohol and drugs. Once the connection was made, the grooming process ramped up, with the men bombarding the girls with texts and phone calls, inviting them to meet up again or attend parties with them.

Once the girls agreed, they were taken to secluded locations – hotels and houses across the Midlands – and sexually abused and raped. The scale and nature of the abuse sickened me to my stomach.

On some occasions, up to six men would participate in the horrific and violent assaults, sometimes filming the attacks on their mobile phones. There was no doubt in my mind that this type of abuse was organised, not just random, by men with an interest in abusing young girls. As the victims began to speak, the true scale and horror of the case became even more evident.[5]

> One 14-year-old who was raped by three gang members 'to the sound of noisy cheering'.
> There were victims who were locked up to prevent them from fleeing.
> A victim was thrown out of a car after being sexually abused.

When the girls said no or tried to refuse their approaches, the men turned to violence, threatening them with hammers or throwing them out of cars. It was no wonder they had been so afraid and reluctant to talk.

The harrowing evidence gathered eventually led to the arrest of thirteen men, aged between twenty-six and thirty-eight. The gang – as it was now accepted to be – faced seventy-five charges relating to twenty-six girls, ranging from rape to intimidating witnesses. In late 2010, almost two years after I had begun my work with Sheila and Debbie, the men faced court in three separate trials, held in secret.

Each of the victims had to stand up in court and tell their story.

Although I didn't attend any of the trials, I followed them closely in the media and through contact with Sheila and Debbie. I knew that cross-examination could be brutal,

---

5 www.dailymail.co.uk/news/article-1345084/Jail-sexual-predators-led-Asian-gang-abused-girls-young-12.html

with the victims' lives picked over in minute detail. This would multiply the trauma and harm experienced. Not only had they already suffered the offences that were committed against them, but they would have to relive them time and again as they went through the court process.

It was heartbreaking, but I was amazed by their courage. Without their testimony, I knew that this gang could have operated under the radar for a very long time. Their bravery, and the courage and persistence of Sheila and Debbie, had made sure this gang was identified and dealt with, and many lives had likely been saved from harm as a result.

It took around ten months to see six men convicted of crimes against the girls[6] and Saddique and Liaqat were identified as the ringleaders of the gang. Saddique, who was aged twenty-seven, was convicted of rape, sexual assault, sexual activity with a child, perverting the course of justice, aiding and abetting rape, false imprisonment and making indecent images of children, and was jailed for a minimum of eleven years. Liaqat, who was twenty-eight, was convicted of rape, sexual assault, aiding and abetting rape, affray, sexual activity with a child and making indecent images of children, and was locked up for a minimum of eight years.

Four other men; Akshay Kumar, Faisal Mehmood, Mohammed Imran Rehman and Graham Blackham were convicted for offences against the girls and a further three men were convicted for charges of perverting the course of justice and cocaine supply.

After the trial, the actions of the gang were described in the media as a 'reign of terror' – one that the victims, Debbie and the team at Safe and Sound brought to an

---

6   www.bbc.co.uk/news/uk-england-derbyshire-11799797

end. Once the sentences had been handed down, Debbie made a statement on the case.

> We welcome the sentences handed down by Judge Head today. They are a reflection of the seriousness of the offences. Abid Mohammed Saddique and Mohammed Romaan Liaqat are sexual predators who preyed on vulnerable girls and young women in Derby.
>
> These men were brought to justice thanks to the bravery of the victims who appeared at the trials of Saddique, Liaqat and their associates. The girls have shown amazing courage and determination to see the men who subjected them to unbelievable cruelty brought to justice.
>
> Officers who are experienced in this type of enquiry were shocked by the scale of abuse some of these young victims faced. This was the most complex case of child abuse the Derbyshire Constabulary has ever faced and the force worked closely with other agencies to bring the perpetrators to justice. We hope that the victims can now move on with their lives and try to put their ordeal behind them.[7]

I had the same wishes as Debbie for the victims. For the police service and my work in the missing, I had other hopes too. I wanted to see human trafficking more firmly on the radar in day-to-day policing, and not just in an international context.

Operation Retriever was clear evidence that human trafficking *was* happening in a domestic setting. The girls in Derby had been taken across city and county borders

---

7   www.capitalfm.com/eastmids/radio/news/local/derby-child-sex-gang-ringleaders-jailed/

for the purpose of being sexually abused, and it shone a spotlight on the fact that it was possible – that it could happen here in the UK, in any town or city, not just internationally. For the first time it was recognised that all that was required was the movement of a person – just across the street was enough. It laid bare the tactics and structures of gangs involved, and it highlighted the things that police should be looking for.

What I'd long thought was finally in sharp perspective: the significance of going missing in relation to serious, horrific and organised crimes was clear, and it was vital that this was understood.

Operation Retriever was considered groundbreaking at the time of its implementation, due to the covert tactics that were used to gather evidence. The tactics that were questioned at the time, and which Debbie received personal criticism for, were ultimately the ones that led to the successful convictions of the gang.

What Debbie did was radical, but it was the right thing to do, and I remain in awe of her courageous approach and desire to bring these criminals to justice and put an end to the abuse. She paved the way for tackling child sexual exploitation in the UK and the convictions in Derby were followed by other notable cases in Rotherham, Bradford and Oxford, to name just a few. Similarly, Sheila continued to drive the agenda forward, later founding the National Working Group (NWG) on Child Sexual Exploitation and being recognised for her work with an MBE.

Where similar gangs were found to be in operation, the majority of subsequent cases were accompanied by findings of failure to recognise or identify this activity that had been going on for many, many years, with countless victims – many of whom we will never know about.

In the Derby case, the convictions brought related to twenty-six girls, but Safe and Sound had information on four times that number of potential victims, and the charity considered that to be just the tip of the iceberg, something I wholeheartedly agree with.

The issue of race was something that drew comment during Operation Retriever, but it was not as prominent a discussion as it has been in subsequent cases. Indeed, not all of the offenders were Asian – one white British man was convicted – and not all of the victims were white. When looking at a case, the ethnicity of a suspect is just another part of their profile as an individual; it is not an indicator that they are more or less likely to be a sex offender. No conclusions could be drawn from the ethnicity of the gang in Derby, and sweeping statements imparting blame on one group were – and remain – unhelpful, inaccurate and harmful. As one senior officer on Operation Retriever told the media: 'Look at the sexual offenders list; it's mainly white men.'[8]

It was around the time of the Derby case that internal trafficking began to be taken seriously and recognised as an issue in the UK. The starkest message that emerged from this and similar cases was that these organised crime groups, exploiting vulnerable children, existed outside of mere rumours and hearsay.

It went on, and it still goes on today. If you think that it doesn't happen in your town, I'm afraid that you are wrong.

As I found out when investigating the causes for the

8   www.bbc.co.uk/news/uk-11819732

Bletchley girls going missing, and again with these cases, it was clear that the need to build better relationships with victims was essential to find information out.

Even at the time of the Derby investigation, the techniques favoured today for interviewing those returning from being missing were not widely in place, despite the fact that their effectiveness was known fourteen years earlier, as I had documented in 'Missing You Already'.

It still baffles and frustrates me to this day that knowledge held for so many years takes so long to come to the fore and become embedded in policing. I often wonder how many victims might have been helped sooner and prevented from suffering if response to change and new techniques was swifter.

Operation Retriever changed that and became a blueprint for dealing with similar cases. Derbyshire Constabulary later established a team dedicated to investigating both child sexual exploitation cases and missing children who had been connected to potential sexual exploitation by intelligence gathered. The initial lack of engagement from the police was fairly typical of policing at that time, mainly due to a lack of awareness of the type of criminality we were uncovering. But step up they did, and the Derbyshire Constabulary response to what they were presented with was excellent.

This provided the resource that had been lacking to develop specialist knowledge, build relationships with other departments, agencies and voluntary organisations involved in the care or management of children, and facilitate information-sharing with them, based on how the Derbyshire Force had worked with Safe and Sound and child protection services.

The resource allowed high-risk cases to be identified earlier and prioritised, and toolkits created ensured that all involved parties were better equipped to deal with the emergence of such cases. These approaches were ones that I had used in my own work in the police and long advocated for, and I was pleased to see them begin to shape national police policy and to witness attitudes towards young people who persistently went missing begin to shift.

Around this time, awareness was growing around the use of the internet to groom children. Through my work in missing children at the Missing Persons Bureau, I had worked with Child Exploitation and Online Protection (CEOP), a world-renowned organisation that focused on protecting children online. I could see that its knowledge and expertise had relevance to missing children and I wanted to make sure that we learned from that expertise.

Shortly after, CEOP took over the bureau's missing children function, with the bureau retaining responsibility for missing adults and national data collection functions. I could understand CEOP wanting to grow and develop, but the move raised many questions for me and was something that I strongly opposed. I agreed that there was a clear need to give particular focus on missing children, but why not add value to what we already had, not break it apart?

What would happen if a child and adult went missing together? Or when a child grew into an adult and continued going missing?

I could see gaps developing that individuals might slip through, and the potential for duplication of effort and resource to make it work. But I could also see the dire need for the continued focus on missing children, so when I was offered the role of Head of Missing Children at CEOP, I accepted.

CHAPTER 8

Abducted

How old are they?

My position as Head of Missing Children at CEOP brought me close to a wide range of initiatives focused on child safety and approaches to finding missing children. By virtue of their age and the circumstances in which they went missing, there were always vulnerabilities and risks that needed to be carefully assessed, to ensure the correct response to their disappearance.

While some initiatives were a success in how well they were recognised by the public and professionals alike, I questioned their efficacy. One particular government scheme developed to improve child safety that I had doubts about was the 'Stranger Danger' initiative.

It had initially been launched in the UK in the 1970s, and had unprecedented success, being adopted widely in schools. By the time I joined CEOP in 2011, it was known and used around the world, but in some quarters, it had met criticisms of failing to keep children safe and creating an unhelpful climate of fear and suspicion.

I worked closely with Lady Catherine Meyer and Geoff Newiss at the charity Parents and Children Together (PACT) and we were convinced it was flawed. Geoff had considerable expertise working in child abduction, and data on these offences showed that stranger abduction was rare.

In the majority of cases, the offender was someone who was known to the child.

Acknowledging this fact, was telling children just to avoid strangers the right message? What did a stranger look like anyway, and were they always bad?

Geoff's extensive research and literature reviews supported our concerns. What's more, studies with children educated in 'Stranger Danger' revealed that, despite having this instilled in them, when a stooge approached them with a dog or story of a lost dog, the child would, almost without exception, unhesitatingly go with this person – so much for an education in staying safe!

In response, Geoff developed a new model, 'Clever Never Goes', in which a friendly robot character 'Clever' educated children to be alert to *anyone* asking them to go somewhere when it hadn't been arranged beforehand.

It seemed to us that for a child to assess whether someone was a stranger and if they represented a threat was too difficult. It also became clear that the 'Stranger Danger' approach deterred children from one of the best safety strategies – going to an adult for help, perhaps with the proviso that they approach a shopkeeper or a person in uniform – as these individuals who might be able to help were all likely to be strangers.

'Clever Never Goes' was employed by many schools, but it struggled to overcome the permeance of 'Stranger Danger' in society's mind, despite it being a classic case of 'something needs to be done' policy producing the wrong results. However, this is gradually changing as people see the benefits of the new approach.

Of course, many of the initiatives that I worked on were responses to high-profile cases that had triggered thoughts about how better solutions could be developed. One was the Child Rescue Alert (CRA), which was launched by Sussex Police in 2002 and later taken under management at a national level and made available to all police forces, something I had been given the task of taking forward and which stayed with me into my role in CEOP.

The CRA had been developed in the aftermath of the abduction and murder of seven-year-old Sarah Payne in Sussex in July 2000. Sarah had disappeared from a cornfield near the home of her grandfather, Terence Payne, and sparked a nationwide seventeen-day search that had been headline news. Her body was found fifteen miles from where she had disappeared and a convicted sex offender, Roy Whiting, was subsequently convicted of her abduction and murder, and sentenced to life imprisonment.

Two years later, Sussex Police became the first force in Europe to launch the CRA initiative, which was based on the American 'AMBER Alert' system, which used news flashes on TV and radio to appeal for help in quickly tracing missing children.

The alerts were reserved for only the most serious and urgent of cases, and only child victims. There were other provisos for its use too. At the time it was established, abduction had to be suspected, there had to be an immediate risk of serious harm or death and there must be sufficient information to enable an appeal to the public to help find the child.

The final point was particularly pertinent, as asking for information from the public would always generate high volumes of calls. The information had to be accurate enough to enable them to be evaluated.

If, for example, the only information was that the offender was an average-looking male driving a white van, there would be no way of filtering out the calls about the wrong white van and man.

On paper it seemed like an appropriate response and useful tool to have in our toolkits when dealing with missing children. Its American counterpart had, after all, been very successful. But put into practice in the UK, it faced some issues.

The CRA had been used by Sussex Police in relation to the disappearance of a young girl from her home. It was initially treated as a missing person case until a twelve-year-old boy came forward, saying that he had seen the child being dragged into a car that was then driven off at speed.

Prompting thoughts of an abduction, a CRA was issued and the media descended on the scene to report on what was happening. However, the following morning, the missing girl was found in a neighbour's house, happily sleeping. The witness had made up the story.

To quote a saying we often use when dealing with missing people and taken from major crime investigation, there had been a failure to 'clear the ground under your feet', meaning dealing with what was close to the last point at which the person was last seen. It also raised the difficulty in knowing when to trust the testimony of a child.

Driving the use of the CRA at a national level presented many challenges, and I'd had my doubts of its efficacy. One thing that struck me from the outset was who would understand what Child Rescue Alert was? AMBER Alert was already reasonably well known on a global level, so I'd suggested that we use that instead, but the idea was vetoed on more than one occasion.

Regardless of its name, I knew the CRA needed work to be more effective. The public needed to know what it was for, and that it should not be overused. It needed to be capable of being activated quickly, and it needed to be able to cope with information that was provided.

The model needed to be national, but scalable to local needs, as publicity should be focused as much as possible on the place where it was needed.

I set up an on-call advisory service in relation to CRA, for all police forces in the UK, with staff drawn from the Missing Persons Bureau and my Missing Children's Team, to offer advice on cases where CRA was a consideration. These included my deputy, Neil Dodds, formerly a detective inspector, and Tony Osbourn, a highly experienced advisor on suspicious missing person cases.

On 1 October 2012, it was my turn to be on call. It was late evening and I was in the conservatory at home when my phone rang. It was one of my contacts in Dyfed-Powys Police, Detective Chief Inspector Shane Williams.

'Charlie, I need your advice,' he said. 'We have a five-year-old girl we are concerned about. We don't know what has happened yet, but we are taking the case very seriously.'

'What do you know at the moment?' I asked.

As Shane outlined the information they had, a shiver ran down my spine. I was used to dealing with countless missing persons cases and I had extensive knowledge of the usual patterns that one might expect to encounter. I couldn't immediately put my finger on it, but this case just felt different.

'Shane,' I said. 'This sounds like a one-in-ten-year case.'

It was only after the words left my mouth that I realised it was ten years since the horrific case of Holly Wells and Jessica Chapman, two young girls who had gone missing in Soham and were later found to have been murdered. I already recognised echoes of that in this case.

I instinctively knew that this was going to hit the head-lines and would be a serious challenge to the police, as well as having a huge impact on the girl's family, friends and whole community.

The missing child was April Jones, a young girl from the Welsh market town of Machynlleth in Powys, in the far west of the country. It was rural, remote and had a population of less than 2,500.

Shane told me that April lived with her family and had last been seen at about 7.15 p.m., playing outside with friends. Her concerned family had called the police at 7.30 p.m., and the only information available regarding her disappearance came from a seven-year-old friend who had been the last to see her near a grey van. The fact that Shane and colleagues at Dyfed-Powys Police had recognised the severity and urgency of the case and called me so early was a very good thing. This was how it was meant to work.

Although the severity of the case was clear, the early stage of my involvement meant there was a greater chance to find her, maybe save her from harm. We were still in the 'golden hour', and we had to take the greatest advantage of that.

The location of the disappearance did present some operational challenges. There was very little in the way of CCTV to aid the search for the vehicle and April. Also, Dyfed-Powys was one of the smallest police forces in the UK. It was nothing like policing a large town or city, where large numbers of resources can be called on and, if necessary, supplemented by those from nearby towns and cities. Any substantial level of support needed would take a long time to get there, so using what was available wisely was essential.

The town is small and in a very rural area with a delightful and extremely close-knit community where news spreads fast, and everyone was more than willing to lend a hand in times of need. Despite other challenges, we were certain that local people would be concerned enough to look for April and share any information that they had with us.

Bearing in mind that a vehicle was the focus of the investigation, we agreed that we would put police officers on roads out of the area, checking vehicles and occupants, effectively creating a 'roadblock' around the town. Of course, a fleeing offender might already be long gone, but what if they weren't?

I believed that using some officers to do this was the right thing to do, even if there was only a slim chance of it delivering a successful outcome. It would also create an interaction with people in the area that could prompt them to share useful information.

As Shane continued to brief me, a tantalising piece of information emerged from an early interview with the young witness.

'She said that April got into the vehicle on the wrong side,' he explained.

The phrase 'got in' captured my attention. It implied some degree of compliance, as opposed to being dragged in kicking and screaming. What did this mean, and why the wrong side of the vehicle?

Did the driver help her up into the driver's side because that was easier than reaching across to the passenger side?

'Do you think we should put the CRA out now, Charlie?' Shane asked.

I considered the possibility. April's case met all the criteria. She was a child, so vulnerable and high risk. There was the potential that this was an abduction and there was a risk of harm to the victim.

The big problem, though, was that while we had photos of April, timings and other information, we did not have clarity around the vehicle. We were still working on the uncorroborated information from a seven-year-old child.

It was essential that we focused on confirming what had happened – remembering to clear the ground under our feet and establish the details. To not get carried away, cover all the bases, and put a solid investigative strategy in place.

If we put the CRA out now, we could be flooded by calls from well-meaning members of the public about any one of thousands of grey vans across the UK, overwhelming the phone lines and possibly taking the focus of the investigation from where it was most needed.

'I think it's too soon, but we should start to make the arrangements to go with it as soon as we need it,' I said to Shane, switching on the TV as we spoke. 'We need more information about the vehicle.'

The screen buzzed to life and I flicked over to Sky News. There was already a breaking news crawler running across the bottom of the screen about April's disappearance: *Police search for five-year-old girl missing from Machynlleth, West Wales.*

The sensation that we were dealing with a one-in-ten-year case rushed over me again. The profile it was already gaining, even in its earliest stages, was further evidence for me. Most missing persons cases barely caused a ripple, but the ones that did tended to embed themselves in the public consciousness, as the Soham case had.

'We should keep the CRA under consideration as the investigation progresses and work through the protocols for implementing it so that we are ready to go,' I said. 'The news is out there; it's on Sky now. People will be looking and they will come forward with information.'

We both knew that the information we needed most was likely to lie in the community.

'We are getting more officers out there speaking to local residents and we are interviewing the young girl,' Shane said.

'Great, keep in touch if there are any developments,' I said.

'I will do. Thanks, Charlie,' Shane said.

With an initial response in place, I started to consider further the information we had available to us. Was it accurate? Could it be corroborated?

Clearly, gathering more information about the van was an absolute priority. There were so many vital questions to be answered. Who was the driver, and why did April get in?

We knew that stranger abductions were statistically rare, so was this someone she knew. Was there an innocent explanation for all this? Although it was hard to think of one, I had to ensure we were keeping an open mind. At this stage, it was as important to eliminate possibilities as to include them in the investigation.

I also had to consider how best to perform my role. Should I start the long journey to Wales to be on hand to assist directly, or stay available on the phone?

Like so many times in my career, I really wanted to be there. It was so much better to hear things as they unfolded and to be able to offer advice in the moment. But it would take me five hours to drive there, and I would be unable to offer a suitable level of support during the journey.

With so many questions still unanswered and being in the critical early part of the investigation, I knew I couldn't afford to be out of contact for such a long period of time.

It was a difficult decision, but I knew it was the right one. My role meant my home was always ready to transform into an investigation room. All of my IT was set up: laptop, VPN for secure internet connectivity, my mobile phone and the landline. I had an office, but in situations like this, I tended to work wherever I was most comfortable or wherever I was when a call came in.

I flicked through the news channels and checked online platforms, keeping an eye on updates being reported in the press and online. As I did, I noticed a torrent of information being shared on social media. Channels like Facebook and Twitter had become far more widely used in recent years, but I'd never seen coverage of a case spread so rapidly and in such volume through these mediums before.

There also wasn't really an existing process for managing it, which concerned me. It was clear to me there was a risk that information essential to finding April might be hidden within the myriad posts and information. We had to make sure we did not miss something important.

In conversations with the investigation team in Wales, we agreed that this was something that needed to be monitored, and officers were allocated the role of sifting through the information and following up any relevant leads, while I did the same thing between calls as I worked through the night.

A few hours passed and we still didn't have any more descriptive information on the van, but coverage was spreading through social media and the news channels like wildfire, and not all of it was accurate.

Bearing this in mind, I picked up the phone to Shane again.

'I think we should launch the CRA first thing in the morning to catch people's attention as they are getting up and looking at the news,' I said. 'That way, they will have accurate information and April's photos.'

Unlike how CRAs were usually used, it was not so much about spreading the information first – that was already out there – as spreading the *right* information and giving a number that the public could call if they knew anything of relevance that could help us to find April.

It was agreed that the CRA would be launched at 8 a.m., assuming that April had still not been found. With the story now a national one, we knew there would be a huge response, so I helped to set up the mutual aid from other police forces that would be needed to deal with the volume of calls we were likely to receive, before heading to bed at about 3 a.m.

After only a few hours' sleep, I was up and back to work again. I'd hoped that there might have been a positive outcome and that April had been found safe and well, but a check-in with the force in Wales confirmed that this was unfortunately not the case.

I made my way into London as there was a demand for my presence there to brief the rest of CEOP and the Serious Organised Crime Agency (SOCA) and determine which further resources were needed to support the local police.

The CRA was launched as planned at 8 a.m. We'd expected a significant response, but even I hadn't been prepared for the volume of calls that flooded in. In the first couple of hours, more than 8,000 calls were recorded on the system.

Many were from people trying out the number, saying they had not heard the information about the case properly, and simply asking what was going on. Others called in, well intentioned but with information that was just not relevant.

Despite the overwhelming response, as I monitored what was coming in, there was nothing new or useful. But with the alert out there, there was even greater interest from the media, and between frequent telephone calls with Dyfed-Powys Police, and meetings with different parts of my organisation, I was despatched around London for media interviews about how the case was developing.

Quite early in my policing career, while working with Thames Valley Police, I had been enrolled on a media training course run by an eminent journalist of the time, intended to make us aware of the risks of talking to journalists, how to prepare for interviews, how to present oneself. The course involved practical exercises based on incidents we had been involved in during our career.

I'd done the odd media interview in the past, but this time it was relentless. It wasn't my favourite part of the job, and I found live broadcasts particularly uncomfortable, but the publicity was an important part of our investigation strategy, allowing us to maintain control of the message.

As well as communicating the salient information and routes for people to get in touch, journalists were also interested in the intricacies of the case, and the challenges we were facing.

Speaking to Channel 4 about the information provided by the seven-year-old witness, I explained the difficulties and delicate nature of interviewing children, rather than adults.

'There are the challenges of how you interview a child to get the right information,' I said. 'And with the time of day that the call came in. You can't interview them through the night.'

I wanted to reassure the public that we were doing everything we could to find April.

'The main thing to start off is the high-profile media response using the Child Rescue Alert system, encouraging people to give their information,' I explained. 'But in the background, there's an investigation ongoing looking at what has happened in the local area, evaluating the information, carrying out searches, examining CCTV. We are engaged in the investigation, and we are pursuing some lines.'[9]

After each interview, I was checking in with the local police and CEOP and SOCA teams in London to ensure that whatever I was sharing in the next was the most up-to-date information, in the hope that it would focus the response from the public.

At a very early stage of the investigation, specialist child safeguarding professionals had been drafted in to speak to the seven-year-old witness who had been the last to see April.

The process was very different to interviewing an adult because, under questioning, children could very easily be led in different directions, their memory could be easily corrupted, or they could feel like they had to say something to please or satisfy the adult.

It was vital that they were encouraged to share the truth without feeling that they were under pressure, under threat or in any way 'in trouble'.

While those interviews were under way, more information was coming in from locals too. One name kept coming up again and again – a 47-year-old man named Mark Bridger.

---

9 www.channel4.com/news/manhunt-for-missing-five-year-old-april-jones

He was known to lots of people in the town, including April, as he had two children who attended the same school as her. It had been confirmed that April had been attending swimming lessons at a local leisure centre while her mum and dad, Coral and Paul Jones, attended a parents' evening at her school, an event that Mark Bridger had also been at.

April had invited a friend – the child witness – to her house from the school to watch a film. After pleading with her parents to let them play outside at night, she was last seen riding a pink bicycle.[10]

Descriptions of Bridger painted a picture of a loner, someone whom everyone knew, but who didn't quite fit in. And another vital nugget of information about him was also revealed.

He owned a left-hand-drive Land Rover.

Suddenly the pieces started to fall into place. Now, the comment made by the young witness about April getting into the 'wrong side' of the car started to make sense. A further piece of information that other children had also been in this vehicle meant this was clearly an urgent line of enquiry. We had to locate Bridger as quickly as possible.

Police officers were informed that he was a suspect in the case and advised to arrest him on sight.

As the hunt for him began, we learned that for a short time he joined other members of the local community who were searching for April, alongside police and various other search and rescue groups who had offered up their services.

The new information gave fresh hope that we would find April alive.

---

10 www.examinerlive.co.uk/news/what-happened-april-jones-murderer-25737032

Less than twenty-four hours after April went missing, Mark Bridger was found by officers. He was out walking when they arrested him on suspicion of abducting her.

After the arrest I received a call from Shane, with some shocking news.

'He told officers that there was a dreadful accident and that he had killed April with his car,' he said.

He explained how the arresting officer had described Bridger as 'an emotional wreck' who had immediately said that he knew what the arrest was about. He'd confessed to the car accident and said that when he checked April that 'there was no life in her, no pulse, no breathing, no response in her eyes'.[11]

I sighed heavily as the information sank in. Now April's parents were going to receive the devastating, life-changing news that April wasn't going to be coming home. This would shatter them, and the whole community that had pulled together to try and find her.

Despite all of their efforts, the fantastic efforts of the tiny Dyfed-Powys Police Force and the various agencies that had worked fast and hard on the case, this wasn't going to have a happy ending.

The thrust of the investigation now had to shift. Where was April's body? Why hadn't Bridger reported the accident? Why had he joined the search when he knew what had happened to her?

A search of Bridger's house was ordered immediately. When officers went into the cottage, they made some gruesome discoveries. Fragments of human bone were found

11 www.dailymail.co.uk/news/article-2322683/April-Jones-trial-I-know-said-Mark-Bridger-police-arrested-him.html

in the fireplace and blood was found in several places, which after forensic examination were found to match little April's DNA.

The case was immediately escalated to a murder investigation and a press conference was called. The detective superintendent leading the case, Reg Bevan, made a statement.

> *Mark Bridger has been arrested on suspicion of the murder of April Jones. He remains in custody at Aberystwyth police station where he continues to be questioned. The arrest does not detract from our efforts to find April and we remain committed to finding her. Her family has been informed of this development and as you would expect they continue to be supported by a family liaison officer. While this is a significant development in the investigation, I once again appeal to the public for information which may help us find April.*

On 6 October 2012, six days after I had received the initial call from Shane at Dyfed-Powys, Mark Bridger was charged with April's murder, as well as attempting to pervert the course of justice and child abduction.

With a murder investigation now under way, I continued to assist as and when my knowledge and expertise was required.

Although it was a horrific and tragic outcome, I couldn't have commended Dyfed-Powys police any more highly on their response to such a serious and fast-moving case. I stepped back, confident that they would work just as tirelessly to ensure that justice was served for April and her family.

When I said to Shane during our initial call that 'This is a one-in-ten-year case', I had been right. It was 10 years since the Soham murders, the last case in the UK that had attracted so much attention. Although I was not involved in that investigation, it was around the time that 'Missing You Already' was published, and I followed it closely as there were some important lessons to be taken from it.

It taught us about potential perpetrator behaviours, as Ian Huntley, the local school caretaker who abducted and killed the girls, joined the search for them, spoke to the police about progress with the case and even became the unofficial media spokesperson for the village. Although not to the same extent, Bridger displayed similar behaviours in April's case, joining public searches for the girl.

The Soham case also highlighted failures in information sharing and cooperation between official bodies. It was only through the publicity about the case that members of the public told the police that Huntley had been a rape suspect in the Grimsby area, something that should have been shared between official organisations.

The case highlighted major flaws in both safeguarding of children and how investigations were run, leading to the Bichard Report, which not only tightened up safeguarding processes, but also led to the introduction of the Police National Database (PND) so that vital intelligence could be processed and shared more effectively between forces.

The report changed the way that large police investigations were run, and the search for April was the largest ever seen in the UK, so what happened in Soham undoubtedly affected our response in Machynlleth ten years later.

Apart from the specialist support from SOCA that resulted from my early engagement, a vast range of other specialist resources were used, including PolSAs, police marine units, experts in searching confined spaces and mines, fire and rescue, urban search and rescue teams, coastguard and mountain rescue teams, as well as specially trained CSI dogs from all over the UK.[12]

The operation covered around 60 square kilometres with 650 search sites and the cost of the investigation was in the region of £8.5 million.

However, despite all these efforts, April's body was never found.

It was just over ten years before there would be a missing person case of similar scale, which attracted the same level of attention of the general public and created a similar media frenzy – the case of Nicola Bulley, who went missing in January 2023. These cases really are one-in-ten-year occurrences.

One element of the investigation into April Jones' disappearance that often draws comment and interest from civilians was Bridger's involvement in the search, joining concerned members to try and find her. The fact is, for police investigators, it is something that is commonly observed.

Some get involved to try to evade capture. By knowing what's happening, where the investigation is going, they can stay one step ahead, or even corrupt evidence. What better way to pull the strings with the evidence than going 'What's happening over there?', and charging over with a hoard of people, trampling the scene and potentially destroying the forensics that are there?

Sometimes, it's just about power and control. Everything from the abduction to the murder, to being in the thick

_____

12 www.dailypost.co.uk/news/north-wales-news/search-april-jones-come-end-2637748

of search activity – the whole thing can be a power trip, standing alongside police and family, all the while thinking: *I know who you are, but you don't know who I am.*

Bridger had been described as a strange character, not quite fitting in with the community, but I don't believe that anyone was prepared for what he actually was.

He had convictions for violence and deception dating back to when he was a teenager, but it was content found on his computer that provided a horrific insight into what led up to April's abduction and murder.

Explicit images of sadistic child sex abuse were found on his laptop, and during the trial in May 2013, it was revealed that he had viewed a cartoon image of a bound girl being sexually abused by an adult just hours before April was abducted.

A tape found in Bridger's video player when police searched his cottage was also found paused at the point of a rape and murder scene in a slasher film. The same scene had been recorded twice on the videotape, which contained no other part of the film.

The closing statements of the trial judge, Mr Justice Griffith Williams, were damning. Sentencing him to life imprisonment with a whole-life tariff, he said:

There is no doubt in my mind that you are a paedophile who has for some time harboured sexual and morbid fantasies about young girls, storing on your laptop not only images of pre-pubescent and pubescent girls, but foul pornography of the gross sexual abuse of young children.

What followed is known only to you but this much is certain – you abducted her [April] for a sexual purpose and then murdered her and disposed of her body to hide

*the evidence of your sexual abuse of her, which probably
occurred on the way from the estate to your home because
there is some sixty minutes of your time which cannot be
accounted for. I cannot infer from the evidence where you
murdered her but if she was alive when you took her to
the house, she died there.*[13]

Although during the investigation I did not have any
contact with April's parents, Coral and Paul, I met them
on several occasions afterwards, one time travelling to
Machynlleth with a colleague from Missing People. The
charity had supported them through the whole ordeal
and in the aftermath, and the couple had become heavily
involved with their work.

The impact that the loss of April had on them was clear.
Coral in particular was always very quiet and understandably carrying an unthinkable amount of sadness, but their
drive to help the families of other missing people since has
been remarkable. The year of April's murder, I joined them
at Missing People's Christmas carol service at St Martin-
in-the-Fields church in London and was privileged to be
asked to do one of the readings.

Dyfed-Powys Police were spectacular in the management
of the case. For such a small force they managed a massive
search and investigation with great professionalism, while
holding the attention of the media from across the world,
working in incredibly testing and challenging circumstances.

They also did what was right for the family by keeping
constantly in touch with them, sharing what they knew,

---

13 www.theguardian.com/uk/2013/may/30/mark-bridger-jailed-
life-april-jones

good and bad, all of which is essential in cases such as these. To this day, I remain proud that I was part of something that was managed so well and hold all involved in high regard.

The tragic outcome of April's case was obviously not what any of us wanted, but using the guidelines, systems and frameworks that were in place, and working collaboratively with other agencies, they did everything right, and everything possible to find April. They could not have done any more.

What the case did illuminate were some limitations and weaknesses of the CRA. In this case it served a purpose, getting accurate information out to the public quickly and effectively, along with details about how to contact the police with information. But not a single piece of critical or even useful information came from the CRA. Everything came from police on the ground in the community.

The fact was that the primary function of the alert – dissemination of information of a missing child – had already been filled by the press and social media, which moved far faster than we were able to.

The media undoubtedly plays a vital part in an investigation, both good and bad. In the early days of my career, using media to publicise a case was sometimes a 'tick box' exercise, simply because there was a section on the missing persons reporting form that asked for a tick to indicate whether the case had been given any publicity. Ticking the box was thought to show that everything possible was being done.

Back then, the police had control over when a press release or conference took place and what information was shared. With no social media and everything in print or as a relatively transient presence on TV or radio, finding that information later was much harder. It was much different to today when everything is findable on the internet and social media, not just for a few days but for years to come.

In missing persons cases there should be no publicity without it being part of a media strategy, which in turn should be part of the investigative strategy. This allows us to determine why it is being done, what is going to be said and through which type of outlet.

The CRA has never been as successful as the American AMBER alert, but I have never been able to pinpoint exactly why. I still question its name and if people actually recognise what it is and wonder if that impacts its effectiveness. Or perhaps the early failure of the system, when the child in Sussex lied about seeing a young girl being snatched from the street, has coloured people's view of information gathered in this way.

Yet there are many examples where the approach employed by the CRA has been successful. One case I worked on in the West Midlands involved a teenage girl being targeted for CSE. She had been missing for several weeks and was being moved from house to house. The local police were at their wits' end, unable to find her.

They turned to me, and working with Missing People, we launched a targeted media campaign in the geographical area where we roughly believed she was being held, through the press and the abundance of big digital screens they had in the area. Within one day she was found, and children's services were able to make interventions to help her.

This wasn't strictly speaking a CRA, as it happened weeks after she had gone missing, where a CRA is intended to be almost instant. But it was the same methodology, and it worked.

It is hard to imagine the challenges of a case like April Jones, with the constant pressure to find answers – born both from a desire to resolve it quickly and also from being in the glare of the media. You have to move quickly, but without going too fast and missing things.

There is also the significant task of managing huge numbers of resources and offers of public assistance with long, relentless working days, and little time to rest in between. Cases like these I have found to be the best and worst of jobs to be involved with.

They show what is possible when things are done effectively, but the ever-changing nature of society means that it inevitably sheds light on where new challenges are arising. April's case was the first that I recall generating so much social media attention.

We had to rise to that challenge as effectively as we could at the time, but once the case was resolved, we had to acknowledge that it was a major problem that was becoming present in more and more cases, of all different natures.

It brought our awareness to the power of social media and the opportunities and challenges that it presented and prompted serious discussion around it. It showed how you could quickly lose control of opinion and the impact speculation could have on an investigation.

CHAPTER 9

Doing Nothing Is Not an Option

*Does the missing person have a physical illness
and need medication?*

In the year following the April Jones case, SOCA was rebranded as the National Crime Agency (NCA), and I became an officer of the new organisation. At the time, people liked to call it the 'British FBI', as for the first time in the UK a national policing organisation would have the power to intervene in local policing issues. This was not envisaged as being something that would be done without a very good reason.

As my career had progressed, I'd been allocated international responsibilities too. During my time at the NCPE, around the time of the Derby CSE case, I'd been involved in the establishment of the North Sea Group, which was intended to provide points of contact in missing cases where it was believed that a person might have entered the North Sea.

Experience had shown that bodies entering the North Sea from the countries that bordered it could reappear on the shores of another country, and there were some patterns to what happened to bodies. For example, a body that went into the water in southern England turned up on a beach in Sweden, or body parts from the north of England would be found in the Netherlands, with similar movements between France, Germany and the Scandinavian countries. The group allowed us to discuss relevant cases and share information when this was a hypothesis.

I'd also been invited to attend international events and organisations, such as the US National Center for Missing and Exploited Children (NCMEC) based in Alexandria, just outside Washington DC. NCMEC was involved with AMBER Alert in the US and I saw it as an opportunity to better understand the inspiration behind the CRA, its implementation, and to learn from those who had made such a success of the initiative in the States, to see how I could take the UK iteration forward.

Delivering training was another area where there was demand on an international level. While at CEOP, I was invited to Jamaica to provide training sessions to the police and other government agencies in relation to missing persons.

Wanting to highlight approaches to the missing from a perspective outside of law enforcement, I asked Claire Hubberstey from The Children's Society to join me and create the training together. I was also fortunate enough for Shelley to be able to accompany me as well, at our own expense of course, so we could enjoy my leisure time together.

The visit was an eye-opening one, not least when we were collected for one appointment in an armoured car. Momentarily, I did wonder why I had agreed to take this on. It was clear that the challenges faced in Jamaica were very different to home. We might have experienced issues with organised crime groups and internal trafficking, but the control that gangs had in Jamaica was shocking, controlling whole transport groups and holding local people to ransom.

Parts of Kingston were spectacular, but it was difficult to observe the large numbers of people living in poverty, in contrast to our luxury hotel, and hear about the exploitation of children, which was on a scale not seen in the UK.

From conversations with organisations there, we learned that many were under the control of local crime gangs and those who weren't struggled to avoid coming into contact with them. The law stated that children could use public transport without having to pay before 7 p.m., but at the time the two main bus companies were operated by the criminal mafia, who would not allow children to board the buses before 7 p.m., so they did not lose out on revenue. In the interim between finishing school and being allowed to board a bus home, they were exposed to the influence of the gangs and at a heightened risk of exploitation.

There were many factors that supported this exploitation, from issues with corruption and far more extreme levels of poverty in the country, to having a homicide rate so high that missing child reports barely made it on to the radar. There was a huge void between what we in the UK accepted as 'normal' and what was accepted as commonplace in Jamaica.

However, there were people there wanting to make change, and the training Claire and I delivered was well attended by police officers, government agencies, schoolteachers, and local NGOs like Hear the Children Cry, a local organisation providing urgently needed services for children and young people in the country. I think we were both pleased to be able to offer a range of practical solutions to some of their challenges.

Because they had a high homicide rate and issues with gang control, these took priority, and they didn't have an effective response to missing children – things like risk assessments and return home interviews – in place. Simply by being there, we raised the profile of missing children and demonstrated how important it was to recognise risk and work with other agencies. We understood that they would not be able to implement everything we had in the UK, or achieve what we considered the gold standard, but the better understanding helped them to improve from where they were and gave them aspirational goals to aim for.

As my international work grew, I began to understand more clearly the importance of being aware of local situations, customs, legal systems and how the country operates. Having global contacts and networks like the North Sea Group to allow working across international borders was of course vital, but what happened when laws, customs and attitudes were so different and didn't align?

Just short of a year into CEOP becoming part of the NCA, a call came in that raised some of those questions. Police in Hampshire were dealing with an unusual missing person case and wanted some advice.

The missing person was a five-year-old boy called Ashya King. He had been diagnosed with a brain tumour and had been recovering in Southampton General Hospital following major surgery seven days earlier.

After the operation, his parents had disagreed with the treatment route advised by doctors at the hospital. From the information shared with me by Hampshire Police, it emerged that his parents, Brett and Naghemeh King, wanted him to have proton beam therapy, which wasn't available in Southampton or anywhere else in the UK.

Doctors had also told them that the treatment would be ineffective on the type of tumour that Ashya had. Despite this, Brett and Naghemeh expressed their continued wishes to take Ashya abroad for proton beam therapy. The doctors did not agree to his being moved out of hospital, so his parents took him away from the hospital without their consent.

According to the information we had, Ashya was in a wheelchair and unable to move or speak, eating only through a battery-operated tube, which the hospital said was expected to run out in the coming hours. It appeared to be an extremely grave situation.

'The parents left the hospital with Ashya at 2.25 p.m.,' my contact in Hampshire Police, Detective Superintendent Dick Pearson, told me. 'The hospital reported them missing to us at 8.35 p.m.'

'Do we have any indication of where they are now?' I asked.

'Not at this time,' he said. 'But we have to find Ashya as quickly as possible. Doctors have told us that being out of hospital for an extended period poses a serious risk to his life.'

As I considered the action we needed to take, a knot tightened in my stomach. Not only was this going to be a race against time, it was going to be an extremely complex case to resolve.

If the family were still in the UK, it would be easy to circulate the details on the Police National Computer, together with an alert to all police forces to look out for the car and its occupants and check their safety if located.

If they were located, the police force in the area where they were found could have a conversation with Hampshire Police to determine an appropriate course of action. If it was necessary, the parents could be arrested, Ashya could be taken into police protection and returned to hospital to receive the treatment he needed.

It was perfectly legitimate to then de-arrest someone as soon it was no longer necessary for them to be detained – in this case, when Ashya was back in medical care.

But if the family had left the country, it would add all sorts of complications.

Anticipating a challenging road ahead, I reached out to some of my missing person contacts in Europe, hoping to smooth the process along. It was an informal network though, and I quickly found that many had moved on. The experience prompted me to think that this was a gap that needed addressing.

But there was little time to ponder the idea further in that moment. We had a strategy to devise, and we had to work out the best course of action for ensuring Ashya's safety.

First of all, we had to deliver a plan that our European counterparts could act on. The challenge was that judicial systems in every country were completely different from those in the UK.

Laws and methods of operation are different, there are language barriers to navigate, and legal processes that need to be followed to request action from another country's law enforcement.

Secondly, we needed to understand where the family might be heading. We knew that the proton beam treatment the family sought was administered in Prague in the Czech Republic, so would they head in that direction? Were there other countries they could travel to for the same treatment? Or did they have another plan completely?

Given the nature of the case, our work would be facilitated through Interpol, the International Criminal Police Organisation, which had 190 member countries. It was decided that a Yellow Notice would be issued. The notice was a notification to police internationally, which alerted them to a missing person. It was intended to help locate missing persons, often minors, or to help identify persons who are unable to identify themselves.

After being posted on the Interpol website and flagged to relevant countries, media interest ramped up.

Hampshire Police made a statement, highlighting the urgency of finding Ashya as soon as possible, and shared a screenshot from the hospital's CCTV showing the couple leaving the hospital with Ashya in his wheelchair.

The force's Assistant Chief Constable, Chris Shead, told media:

> From what we know, it is vital that Ashya's condition mandates that he is fed in that particular way. Time is running out for this little boy. We need to find him, and we need to find him urgently.
>
> It is our dearest hope that his parents will hear this appeal, they will recognise the gravity of the situation Ashya is in medically and they will take him to a hospital. But we will continue to look until we find him.[14]

Before long, headlines were splashed across national and international newspapers.

Interpol issue global alert to find missing Ashya King

UK police warn: Feeding tube of missing boy runs out today

Five-year-old boy with brain tumour 'kidnapped' from hospital by parents

---

14 www.independent.co.uk/news/police-in-race-against-time-to-find-seriously-ill-boy-9698442.html

Eventually, news emerged of the family's whereabouts. Ashya, his parents and their six other children had boarded a car ferry to the port of Cherbourg in France at about 4 p.m. and disembarked some hours later.

Police investigators found that the family had a property in Spain, which was put under surveillance by the Spanish police. As a result of the media coverage, members of the public also made contact and gave information about a sighting of their car and details of a hotel that they were planning to stay at.

As part of the EU at the time, we were able to make use of the Schengen Information System, through which we could alert all European Police to details of the case, from descriptions of Ashya, his family and the registration number of the car they were believed to be travelling in.

Given the circumstances of Ashya being taken without the consent of the hospital, his parents' determination to follow their own decisions about his treatment and the information we had about the urgency of his getting medical attention, we had to work out what would happen in the event of the parents being found.

It was probable that once they were located, they would not go willingly with police, or allow Ashya to be taken to hospital.

We had to have a response that gave police in Europe powers to intervene and ensure that the correct action was taken.

But we couldn't just send an email out to all the European police forces saying, 'Can you detain these people if you see them?' – it was much more complex than that.

By this time, a full major incident room had been set up by Hampshire Police. I was there, together with colleagues from the NCA, to find the correct course of action. While not wanting to turn this into a criminal investigation, we needed to put something in place that ensured Ashya would receive proper treatment as soon as the family were intercepted.

Everyone was keen to share their thoughts and concerns as we planned our next steps.

The main concern was for Ashya's wellbeing. Medics were insistent that if he did not get treatment soon, his life would be at risk.

The Interpol Yellow Notice alerted countries to the fact a person was missing, but it didn't carry the urgency or requirement to act that an AMBER Alert or Child Rescue Alert did. It also did not give law enforcement in other countries the power to take action.

That would be at the discretion of each local police force.

'It is asking a lot of them to take action on the say-so of another country,' someone correctly pointed out.

Collectively, we were edging towards applying for a European Arrest Warrant to ensure that action was taken.

We knew that doing this was likely to prompt some adverse reaction, but saving Ashya's life was of paramount importance and something had to be done. It wasn't an easy decision, but policing never was easy.

The final decision was taken at the highest levels. We would try to secure a European Arrest Warrant, which could only be done through the Crown Prosecution Service (CPS) in the UK.

Without the warrant, any police officer intercepting the parents would find it difficult to detain them if they chose not to cooperate.

With the clock ticking away, an application was put in. The information we were receiving from those who had been in charge of Ashya's treatment was that the actions of his parents were reckless and dangerous to his health, tantamount to neglect.

We nervously awaited the response from the CPS, knowing that if it was denied, we didn't have an effective fall-back plan. All we would be able to do is hope things went OK if the family were intercepted.

Thankfully, based around this information, the CPS evaluated the circumstances and granted our request to seek the arrest of the parents on suspicion of child neglect. The warrant was issued.

This meant that police officers in any European country could now arrest the parents and detain them in police custody. But the approach was met with criticism from the public, with many thinking that it was too heavy-handed, and that the family was only acting in what they believed to be the best interests of their child.

It was an extremely difficult situation. On the one hand, I could see how the approach could be viewed in this way. Hampshire Police themselves had conceded that it was unclear if a crime had actually been committed.

But a child's life hung in the balance; it would have been wrong of us to not do whatever was necessary to protect him.

It would also be extremely foolhardy for us not to believe what the medical authorities were telling us. We were not experts in treating brain tumours, so we had to defer to their greater knowledge of the condition, its treatment and the specifics of Ashya's health.

Our focus was on saving Ashya, and we had to be guided by that expertise.

When the warrant was issued, ACC Shead made a further statement, acknowledging the public response and explaining the decision.

'I can confirm we have obtained a European Arrest Warrant. What that will do is, when we find Ashya and his family, it will allow us to talk to his parents about what happened,' he explained. 'It purely gives us the power to arrest, and then we'll be able to speak to them.'[15]

It wasn't about punishing the parents. It was all about making sure that Ashya was safe.

Following a lead that suggested the family had connections to Marbella in Spain, the family had been spotted in their Hyundai people carrier by police in Velez-Malaga, a town about an hour to the east of Marbella.[16]

At about 9 p.m., UK time, on 30 August 2014 – two days after they had fled the hospital in Southampton – they were arrested and taken into custody by Spanish police,[17] while Ashya was immediately taken to hospital for treatment.

He was described as being in good condition and not showing any visible signs of distress, which was a great relief to us all.

It emerged that the couple had checked into a hostel about fourteen miles away from Velez-Malaga, where they had left their six other children. They had gone to Spain with the intention of selling a property to raise some of the estimated £90,000 required to pay for the proton beam therapy.

We had achieved our aim of ensuring Ashya's safety and getting him back to a hospital. But with the couple being

---

15 www.theguardian.com/society/2014/aug/30/parents-missing-ashya-arrest-warrant

16 www.nbcnews.com/news/world/ashya-king-case-missing-boy-brain-tumor-alive-spain-parents-n192521

17 www.theguardian.com/society/2014/aug/31/ashya-king-found-spain-parents-arrested

held under a European Arrest Warrant, we were now bound by following the associated processes. Where we could simply 'de-arrest' the couple in the UK, under our domestic power of arrest, the only way for the process to be resolved in Europe was through a hearing in a court of law.

In the days that followed, Ashya's parents were not allowed to visit him, and his sibling, Danny, was only allowed to go and see him with judicial permission. Prior to that, his entire family had been banned from seeing him, and a guard had been stationed outside his ward.

Hampshire Police was heavily criticised for criminalising what some members of the public described as a family matter. A petition to have them released was circulated online, gathering some 200,000 signatures from around the world. Even the UK's prime minister at the time, David Cameron, got involved.

While making it clear that it was not the government's place to tell the police what to do, he made a plea for 'an urgent outbreak of common sense' and the couple's release. His deputy, Nick Clegg, also spoke on the case saying that it was 'not appropriate' to 'throw the full force of the law' at the family.[18]

On 2 September, the CPS dropped the case against the couple, who were subsequently released.

This was an extremely difficult case, technically and emotionally. Having to weigh up the evidence presented by medical professionals to assess the risk to Ashya and decide on an effective and proportionate response was one

18 www.standard.co.uk/news/uk/parents-of-ashya-king-to-sue-hospital-and-police-over-cruelty-claims-9706118.html

challenge. Navigating the complex nature of making that response possible to deliver through foreign police and legal systems was another.

It was not a perfect solution. As ACC Shead said himself in a statement after the arrests, 'There are no winners in this situation.'[19] But it did achieve the aim of getting Ashya safely back to a hospital.

On the day of their arrest, a YouTube video was posted by Ashya's brother, Naveed, showing Ashya's dad, Brett, explaining the couple's decision to take their son out of hospital and seek medical help abroad. It showed Ashya connected by tubes to feeding supplements and he spoke about how they had been labelled as kidnappers and accused of neglect.

Thinking about my own son, Tom, and being a father myself, I wonder how I would have responded in a similar situation.

It is important to recognise the dreadful stresses that Ashya's family were suffering. I have no doubt they were doing what they thought was right at the time, and I sympathised with them in their desire to ensure their son's future.

However, in the incident room, we were dealing with information that stated that a child's life was in danger, and we had to find a solution to reconcile that.

If that clarity did not exist and Ashya was not afforded urgent medical attention, our information told us that he could die.

We were heavily criticised. On one occasion after the case, I was even taken to task by a Member of the European

---

19 www.theguardian.com/society/2014/aug/31/ashya-king-found-spain-parents-arrested

Parliament, who tackled me after I had spoken at a meeting in the parliament building in Strasbourg. He had berated me for the police action, asking why we had to do what we did, repeating much of what had been stated by other politicians.

In fact, a lot has been said and written by lawyers, politicians, journalists and other experts that criticise what we did and alleges misuse of lawful powers. I have listened to and read many of these criticisms, but one thing is missing, and that is any suggestion of what an alternative solution or course of action might have been.

I remain satisfied that we made the best choice we could in the circumstances, resulting in Ashya being placed back into qualified medical care with confirmation that he was okay.

Happily, he did also eventually receive his proton beam therapy. In 2018, it was reported that he was cancer-free and doing very well, which I was very pleased to learn.[20]

It was not the first or last time I would encounter the challenges presented by missing person cases that crossed international borders and featured different cultural approaches.

At one conference, hosted with partners and colleagues to mark the launch of a system that enabled the mutual recognition of missing person alerts from other countries, I noticed a very large man bearing down on me.

At the first opportunity he cornered me, and I realised immediately that he was not in the best of humour. He announced that he was a police officer from an Eastern

20 www.news.sky.com/story/ashya-king-may-be-cancer-free-after-pioneering-proton-therapy-11274109

European country and had recognised my name from a case I had been involved in.

'Why did you interfere?' he demanded. 'The father had the children.'

At first, I didn't have a clue what he was talking about, so I was both puzzled and intimidated. But as he continued it became clear that he was referring to a case of parental abduction from the UK, which I had dealt with while working for the Missing Persons Bureau.

True to my nomadic working style, the call had come in while I was walking from Euston Station in London to St Pancras, to catch a train to my next meeting. It was a police officer asking for advice about how to deal with an international parental abduction, and if we could track where a father was taking his children.

It emerged that a father had taken his children from their mother against her wishes and left the country. This is a criminal offence in the UK, but not in all countries, making it extremely complex to deal with.

Working on the move, I was able to advise and initiate some actions from other UK agencies and we managed to trace their movements across the English Channel, through Belgium and further north across Europe, eventually going to the father's home country. This then resolved into long drawn-out legal processes to confirm the welfare of the children and to try to get them returned home to their mother.

It turned out that parental child abduction was not a criminal matter in the police officer's country. From his – and the country's – standpoint, the children were with their father, and that was all that mattered.

I did try to calmly explain to this man that we viewed it somewhat differently in the UK, but it did not alleviate his anger and we parted ways from this rather incongruous meeting.

Another case, some years later, concerned the taking of three children from the UK to Costa Rica by their mother. I was contacted for advice on this case and had tried to make sure that all the legal processes were understood and followed, but working with such a distant country was not easy and the case began to stretch out.

Then, one day, I received a call from the UK-based police officer who was involved in the case and had been my primary contact.

'Hello, Charlie,' he said excitedly. 'I have sorted it!'

'How did you do that?' I asked.

'Well,' he explained, 'I managed to find a cop in Costa Rica and gave him a ring to ask if he could do anything. He just rang back to say he had been to the hotel and grabbed the mother and kids and took them to the police station.'

'How did he get them to do that?' I asked.

'I believe he persuaded her with his gun,' he said.

I winced at the thought. It was the desired outcome, but not exactly the approach I had anticipated, nor what I would have advised. However, the children had been located and taken to a place of safety, eventually returned to their father and court proceedings resulted in offenders being sent to prison.

Not all cases have such resolutions. Recently, I was asked to advise a family where a mother had taken her daughter out of the UK to Sweden, in circumstances that meant she was committing an offence of parental child abduction.

The case was dealt with under the Hague Convention, going before an international court and a ruling being made that the child should be returned to the UK. I made various suggestions about actions to take and organisations that could help, speaking to someone I knew in the Swedish police to help smooth the process.

With the court ruling being in place, I was confident that the mother and child would be located, and the order of the court carried out. But I was shocked to find that neither the police nor the prosecutor wished to take any action – how could that happen when there was a lawful ruling in place?

At the time of writing, the case is continuing to drag on – a terrible thing for the family and the child involved, who is likely to have suffered significant mental harm as a result of the experience.

This is the challenge of dealing with abduction, particularly family abduction. It has many facets, and the law varies from country to country. There are different cultural attitudes and approaches. Even in the UK there are different types of offences. In Scotland, there is an offence of 'plagium' – the theft of a child below the age of puberty – that does not exist elsewhere.

It is also sometimes the case that police officers consider such cases to be civil matters, despite there being legislation that makes it a crime.

In cases like these, it is difficult, if not impossible, to achieve a perfect outcome.

When the police are presented with circumstances where information is based on the expertise of a professional person, or any other evidence that says that a child's life is in danger, they are bound to take action to safeguard that child.

However, the circumstances do not always fit conveniently within the law as it is written – particularly where international laws come into play – and a compromise must be found to locate the child as soon as possible.

Many people who are asked to make decisions in critical situations like this are subject to scrutiny and review, and quite rightly so. But I do believe any criticism must be made in light of what information was available at that time.

This is why I have always told officers to record their decision-making and what facts it is based on at the time. Hindsight is a wonderful thing but can fuel ill-informed criticism if based on information that was not known at the time.

The simple fact is, in critical situations where a life is at risk, or there is a threat of harm, doing nothing is not an option.

Even if the action you take causes upset. Policing is often like that.

CHAPTER 10

County Lines

Have they been missing before?

In my role as Head of Missing Children for CEOP, I was a regular visitor to the Home Office, Department of Education and many other government agencies, and sometimes required to attend meetings at the House of Commons, House of Lords and 10 Downing Street.

The journey that I had started with the PRAS project and writing 'Missing You Already' more than a decade earlier had taken me to places I'd never expected – that I had scoffed at the notion of, no less.

But while my life had changed immeasurably, I was struck by how many of the same challenges we still faced when it came to working in missing persons, and how long it took for people to see what some of us embedded in the area recognised so much earlier.

It was a pattern in policing that I saw time and again, when new ideas, solutions and different ways of working were presented.

The highest volume of missing persons we were seeing was between the age range of 12–17 years, with a considerable proportion of these being children in care. When I had first taken the position at CEOP in 2011, I used my position as lead in missing children to build on my earlier work to develop solutions that might reduce the high volume of these youngsters who were going missing, and improving processes for identifying those who were at high risk of harm and exploitation.

The challenge we faced was balancing the large numbers of missing young people and the impact they had on policing, with being able to identify the indicators of serious harm and responding in a proportionate manner. I could see that there was a real need to get to grips with the difference between being a missing person and 'testing boundaries'.

My research had led me to a contact in Sussex Police, Inspector Jon Gross, who was also passionate about the issue. He was seeking to reduce the number of cases of missing young people that was consuming vast amounts of his force's time and resources, making more time available for those that required a specific focus.

His approach was radical. Instead of all cases being reported missing, subject to sensible control measures, some cases were being reported as 'absent'.

The theory behind it was that this constant ebb and flow of young people, who were largely in care, did not warrant a full missing person investigation on every occasion that a report was made.

When an individual was reported absent, the police would be notified. The situation would then be monitored by both the police and those responsible for them – a social worker or care home, for example.

They would be responsible for looking for any indicators of risk or harm, such as patterns of behaviour, people they associated with and places that they went to. If there were concerns, the case could be escalated to missing person. If not, the information would be added to what was known about the young person in case any patterns of behaviour arose.

On a small, single-force scale, I could see this was working. Time spent on missing person cases of this nature was reduced, but with proper monitoring to ensure that there was not an unreasonable risk to the child.

But could it work nationally? I knew it was potentially controversial. When a child was missing, it was important to understand why they had gone and what they were doing, and some saw it as too great a risk to not fully investigate. On the other hand, we knew that many children who were reported missing were simply testing boundaries, late home or wanting time out from their care home.

But the approach could enable a clearer focus on high-risk cases without compromising the safety of children. Despite the potential challenges, I wanted to try it out, so I drew up a model for how it could work on a national level.

My gut was telling me that this model could really work, but I hadn't wanted my personal views to interfere. I decided that the trial should be managed by an appropriate independent person who was based in the Home Office. But, to my horror, after we had agreed the plan in my initial meeting, the appointed project lead decided to abandon all further consultation and simply go ahead with the new model.

I knew the consultation process might have been an uncomfortable one. I had been prepared to hear views that did not agree with my own, but to not take the views of other organisations into consideration at all was a huge mistake.

Involving relevant people in the creation of the process meant that they would all have had a stake in what was achieved. Instead, the process was just passed down from above and as a result there was a great deal of discontent, and it was attacked by many people and organisations.

It was not something I was used to, and by my standards it was a failure. I was deeply disappointed, not least because I had truly believed it was a solution for a serious problem plaguing so many forces at the time.

It turned out that people were once again just a little behind us on the uptake. Shortly afterwards, the 2013 ACPO Interim Guidance on missing persons, of which I was the author, was published. Following the usual robust consultation and insight processes, a decision was made and approved by ACPO to change the definition of missing to include the 'absent' category, and the interim guidance was commissioned to inform police forces of the changes to existing guidance that would come as a result. For me the guidance was absolutely vital because, historically, I had seen high numbers and repeated instances of young people going missing from care create a negative attitude and blindness to the potential risks these young people faced.

But there were complexities in missing persons that needed to be considered and a balance that needed to be found.

In my early days of policing, I had attended a training course with officers from different parts of the country. Inevitably, stories were exchanged, and officers based in Liverpool complained about teenagers running away from children's homes in North Wales to their city.

'It's a nuisance having to drive them back to the home, then they go missing again,' they'd said, annoyance with the situation clear.

At the time, there was a wide and prevailing attitude of irritation regarding young missing people who would turn up again with no explanation for why they'd gone off and worried everyone. The usual outcome was they'd get a telling-off, from both police officers and those responsible for them, for causing worry and distress, and sometimes even be blamed for wasting everyone's time.

This was, of course, extremely unhelpful, and demonstrated the lack of understanding of what going missing really meant and how to respond to it.

Nobody had bothered to gain the trust of those children who were ending up in Liverpool, to try and find out why they were running away. It was only years later, following a three-year, £13-million investigation, that it was revealed that many of them had been subjected to years of physical and sexual abuse in care homes in Clwyd and Gwynedd, in what came to be known as the North Wales child abuse scandal. Those poor children had been running away from abuse and rape, only to be told they were a nuisance, and taken back to the care homes by the police to be subjected to more of the same.

The two foregoing accounts might appear to be contradictory but illustrate some of the challenges faced when assessing what should be done. When faced with a high volume of missing people, you have to try and manage resources and deal with it in an effective way, but at the same time you cannot fall into the trap that police in Liverpool did, dismissing everything out of hand.

The absent category is an opportunity to manage resources while ensuring adequate attention is paid. Every instance of someone going missing should be considered and evaluated to determine the correct response, which might be monitoring the situation (absent) or actively investigating it (missing). That those who are responsible take a professionally inquisitive interest is important.

Where there were repeated instances of young people going missing, there was *always* a reason and as I was learning, it usually involved them being at risk of exploitation or coming to some form of harm, even if they didn't recognise it themselves.

Sometimes a single case or incident could reveal countless others, and unravel a whole network of criminal activity, as we'd seen in Derby with Operation Retriever. But it wasn't always child sexual exploitation at the root of it. We were starting to recognise that children and young people were being exploited for other criminal means too.

Still travelling extensively around the UK in my role with CEOP, I was working with police forces and other agencies involving missing young people. One call took me to Croydon in South London to review the case of a missing teenage girl who had not been seen for several weeks.

'We've tried everything and we're running out of ideas,' the investigation team lead said. 'Can you see if there's anything we've missed or offer any suggestions?'

On reviewing the case, I could see they'd done a good job, following all recommended steps effectively. Apart from repeating and enhancing some of the actions already taken, there was little advice I could offer. With the girl still not found, other routes began to be explored.

'Perhaps we should escalate to a murder investigation?' the investigation team lead said.

Given the time that had elapsed since her disappearance, I could understand why that might be considered, but I wasn't so sure. There were some addresses in Central London that I believed were worthy of ongoing attention, as they had been identified as places where the girl might be accommodated.

If that was the case, I knew it was likely that she was being exploited in some way. It didn't feel like the right time to escalate to a murder investigation.

'Let's focus on these addresses first and put a good strategy in place for managing her return,' I said, still hopeful that she might be found.

By good fortune, she was. Police located her at one of the addresses on our watch list a day or so later. A robust return strategy in place as I had suggested, officers and children's services spent time building her trust and encouraged her to talk about what had happened to her.

As I'd suspected, she had been persuaded to go to the address with some older men and had then been exploited. As was my normal course of action in cases such as these, I had conversations with contacts within other organisations and charities, such as Missing People, to see if they knew anything about the missing girl.

In this case they did not, but it did trigger a conversation about what they had noticed happening in that area and there were overlaps with what we knew about this case. I extended these conversations to other organisations and a much richer picture started to emerge.

We began to map the movements of missing teenagers around Croydon – not just girls, but boys too. Compared to other areas, the number of children going missing from Croydon was unusually high.

We noted links to other locations in the South East and areas across Central London, and realised that many missing from Croydon were visiting these areas, while young people missing from those areas were being found in Croydon.

What's more, a significant number of children reported missing in other parts of the country, including the West Midlands, the South West and large towns and cities in the North of England, were being found in Croydon too. What was it that was bringing these missing teenagers to the town?

It looked to me like much more organised activity than we were used to seeing. There was clearly a problem, something untoward going on, but what and who was driving it?

There was an issue there had been murmurings of in various parts of the country.

County Lines.

It was being talked about mainly as a London problem, when I would attend the quarterly briefings at the Mayor's Office for Police and Crime (MOPAC) briefings at City Hall. It was there that I met Tony Saggers, who was the head of drugs threat and intelligence at the NCA and leading on County Lines.

Tony was another of those rare people who identified and passionately believed in an obscure issue that needed greater recognition, and what I learned from him about this issue led me to believe that it could be what we were looking at in Croydon.

Taking learnings from past cases, I ensured that all relevant agencies were involved, calling a meeting with senior police staff and the head of children's services in the area to consider a strategy. We agreed that there were reasons for concern, but collectively we were still not sure what those concerns were.

Over the course of the meeting, we concluded that it was possible that the missing children were being exploited for criminal purposes. I recommended some in-depth data analysis, sharing information from all agencies, that would either prove or disprove that theory.

With that agreed, I reviewed potential approaches. The traditional method for monitoring the riskiest missing children was to have a list of the top ten most prolific individuals, as reported to the police, give particular focus to them, and try to find an appropriate response to their behaviour.

However, this was a constantly changing list and tended to focus on the individuals and their circumstances. Might that be too narrow a focus for this investigation?

I decided to change our approach from the traditional to one based on the belief that there were common factors behind the missing children. Croydon Police generated a list of the top ten riskiest missing children – the ones that went missing most prolifically – on a weekly basis. I decided that would be our starting point.

'Pick any of the recent top ten missing,' I told my analyst, Mike Constantinou. 'Look for common links between all of the reports – instances of people they met, places they visited, transport they used and *any* other common factor that appears, then analyse those common points and see what you can find.'

My theory was that if there was exploitation going on, the same people would be involved, using the same addresses and methods of transport. If we identified those common points, I believed we'd reveal many more missing children and whatever was behind their disappearances.

Mike set to work, but it wasn't long before he met some resistance. Despite our approach being sanctioned by the head of children's services and senior police officers, middle managers were blocking Mike's work, too frightened to share information in case of some imagined repercussions.

I was astonished. Government guidance on the subject clearly stated: '*Sharing of information between practitioners and organisations is essential for effective identification, assessment, risk management and service provision. Fears about sharing information cannot be allowed to stand in the way of the need to safeguard and promote the welfare of children and young people at risk of abuse or neglect.*'

It was there in black and white. Fears about sharing information should not be allowed to stand in the way of safeguarding and promoting child welfare. But here we were, with children's lives at risk or being damaged, all because we were not allowed access to much of the information that was available. It was deeply frustrating.

I should not have been surprised, though, as it was reasonably common for the fear of data sharing to inhibit proper practices, something that had been cited in many serious case reviews, including those relating to the Soham murders, which had highlighted failures in information sharing and cooperation between official bodies, and the Baby P case, which found that the child had been failed due to the 'completely inadequate'[21] approach by the majority of professionals who had been involved in the case.

Despite these limitations, though, patterns did start to emerge from the data Mike *was* able to access and it seemed to indicate the occurrence of County Lines.

County Lines were essentially a drug-dealing network. An operation would be based in major towns and cities, with drug-running 'lines' set up to send drugs out to smaller

---

21 www.theguardian.com/society/2010/oct/26/baby-p-death-should-have-been-prevented

towns within the orbit of the major town or city at the centre of the network.

The 'line' referred to in 'County Lines' was a mobile phone that a drug dealer used to take orders and sell drugs. Once an order was placed, they would send the goods via child couriers to the purchaser in the other town.

The patterns that Mike and I were seeing mirrored this kind of network and activity.

The victims were vulnerable young people, enticed and entrapped by the same methods employed in other cases of child exploitation that I'd seen – gifts, brainwashing, fear, coercion and physical violence. It was a callous exploitation that took advantage of children being an expendable commodity, and one that was less noticeable to the authorities than using adult drug mules. They were used and abused for nothing more than to further the ends of the drug dealers at the top of the network.

As their networks, profits and power grew, the more young victims suffered.

The persistently missing people that we were finding connected to these County Lines were badly damaged. They were being sucked into this violent and dangerous world for an array of reasons – escape from abuse, depravation, threat of violence and fear – and left with a future that could only lead to further criminality, if nothing was done to stop it.

It wasn't just the young people being coerced into running drugs that were experiencing harm. Another characteristic of County Lines was a form of exploitation called 'cuckooing'.

Taking its name from the lifestyle of the cuckoo, which lays its eggs in another bird's nest and leaves them to raise its young once they hatch, drug dealers identified vulnerable people, often living in social housing, 'persuading' them to let them use their home as a base for their drug dealing. Once they were in, they'd be near impossible for the vulnerable resident to get rid of.

When a drug dealer recognised that his local area had reached saturation point, or identified new opportunities in another town, this is how they'd go about sorting their new base. A new foothold in place, child couriers from all around would bring drugs there to be sold, with the main dealer remotely maintaining total control on the house via his mobile phone.

All the indicators were there, yet we were still struggling to get people in the police service to accept that was what was happening. In my lead role in this investigation, I had to work with the team in Croydon and other involved agencies to prove there was an issue.

Once again, cases were being viewed in isolation, with the bigger picture being overlooked.

When I was supporting the investigations, County Lines was not only less well known, it also wasn't really recognised. There was some progress in addressing the problem, but it was painfully slow, in part on account of that lack of understanding and acceptance. However, thanks to the groundwork we had laid, some arrests were eventually made, albeit after I had resigned from CEOP.

I might not have seen the ultimate outcome of that work, but I do believe it helped to raise the profile of the issue of County Lines. It is now a widely recognised form of criminality and exploitation, with specialist teams and units investigating it and many successful prosecutions being made as a result – a simple internet search for 'County Lines convictions' will return hundreds of results.

At the time of writing, a gang of four men have just been jailed for more than fourteen years following a Met investigation that revealed a County Line running from Croydon to Dundee.[22]

The investigation began in November 2022, sparked by concerns raised by officers regarding a sixteen-year-old child who had gone missing. When they were located in Dundee, it was also discovered that the four suspects had also travelled to the city around the same time.

The connections had been made, so the problem could be dealt with.

Speaking to people who go missing and return has, to me, always been the most basic and effective part of managing missing persons, particularly in cases of young people who repeatedly go missing, and I believe it should be universally implemented.

This was included in the statutory guidance on children who run away or go missing from home, published by the Department for Education in 2014:

When a child is found, they must be offered an independent return interview. Independent return interviews provide an opportunity to uncover information that can help protect children from the risk of going missing again, from risks they may have been exposed to while missing or from risk factors in their home.

The interview should be carried out within 72 hours of the child returning to their home or care setting. This should be an in-depth interview and is normally best carried out by an independent person (i.e., someone not

22 www.londonnewsonline.co.uk/gang-of-four-jailed-in-county-lines-sting-after-missing-croydon-teenager-found-in-scotland/

*involved in caring for the child) who is trained to carry
out these interviews and is able to follow up any actions
that emerge. Children sometimes need to build up trust
with a person before they will discuss in depth the reasons
why they ran away.*

I was part of the working group that wrote that guidance,
which is statutory – meaning that it is a legal requirement.
Yet I am frequently shocked and disappointed to find that
it is not always implemented across the country.

The fact that when it is done, it identifies the reasons a
child is going missing and enables interventions to be made
to prevent or reduce harm, should be a good enough reason
to implement the guidance. There are financial benefits too.
Research from the University of Portsmouth found that the
basic cost of investigating a case was between £1,325.44
and £2,415.80, with costs for serious cases climbing much,
much higher.

Multiply that by the number of missing person incidents
reported to the police, as shown in data from the Missing
Persons Unit in 2021/22 – 294,220 reports. Other research
from Australia suggests that for each missing person, twelve
other people are impacted by their disappearance, a huge
human cost per missing person.[23]

Effective and routine return home interviews could miti-
gate these costs by identifying the reasons a child is going
missing and tackling them, therefore stopping them from
going missing again, and potentially preventing others from
doing so as well.

---

23 www.researchgate.net/publication/260401235_Missing_Persons_
Incidence_Issues_and_Impacts

It has been evidenced time and again; if you remove the root problem, people stop going missing.

Sadly, as is the case with all missing person prevention, return home interviews are an invest-to-save option and putting money up front to make a later saving is not very attractive, which is one of the reasons why it does not get done. There is a far greater preference for saving money by making cuts. It is still such an enormous missed opportunity in many cases.

Friends working at the charity Missing People have shared numerous stories about their return home interview scheme and how it has identified problems and enabled solutions for missing children.

One case that was shared with me was a boy who had started going missing from home where he lived with his parents. He was exhibiting disruptive behaviour when he was at home, like punching holes in doors and walls.

He went missing several times and was referred to the scheme as no one could understand what was motivating his behaviour. Slowly and painfully, over a series of meetings, he began to talk about his life at home and it emerged that his father was abusing him. He was punching things in frustration and running away to escape.

We often think about runaways as being at risk but for some of them, sadly, they are safer when they have run away. Like the children in North Wales – how often have we returned victims of abuse to their abusers through not understanding why they are behaving as they are?

In cases of child sexual exploitation, for many years the victims we were seeing were almost always girls. But, again, this was because we weren't looking well enough into the reasons for certain behaviours in boys. There were, in fact, many more male victims than we previously understood.

We realise now that this was probably caused by the greater stigma around homosexuality in those days. While many of the male victims were not gay, they felt extreme guilt at what was happening with their abusers, they did not want to think of themselves as being gay and found it much harder to disclose to the authorities.

For reasons such as these, the importance of continued effort to build trust and understanding cannot be under-estimated. It is this which enables victims to speak out.

Through my own learnings, I have encouraged this approach in many difficult cases I have dealt with during my career and it has only ever had positive results; better support for the victims, a greater understanding of their problems, and offenders being caught and punished.

Another highly complex issue raised in both working with Safe and Sound on the Derby CSE investigation and in the Croydon County Lines cases was the issue of judging if someone was a victim or an offender.

In the early days of my involvement, it was widely believed that victims were making a lifestyle choice to become involved in these types of activities. Even the terminology I used in 'Missing You Already' around 'child prostitution' reflected the language and also attitudes of the time. Reading it now makes me shudder.

There was a suggestion that there was some complicity in the victims' actions. But we must remember that, for them, life is almost intolerable. They have been lured or coerced into these situations, perhaps being raped by different men each day, or forced under threat of violence to peddle drugs hundreds of miles from home. Some are later found to be actively recruiting other young people into the same cycle of abuse.

According to legal definitions, they were committing criminal acts. Does this make them an offender?

But there was another side to consider, as one young victim's simple explanation clearly illustrates: *'I am being forced to have sex with lots of men every day and if I can recruit someone else, I can have some time off.'*

This is also seen in County Lines, where victims find themselves physically and mentally exhausted from having to travel the length of the country to deliver drugs, often being threatened with physical harm to themselves or a loved one, should they not comply. Sometimes their only chance for some respite is to recruit another youngster into the role, to relieve some of the burden on them.

The truth is that the blame and responsibility lie squarely and solely with their inhuman abusers, who exploit by any means they consider will work, whether it be bribery through the giving of gifts, raping their victims or using other physical violence.

We cannot forget the age of some of these victims. Some that we encountered were as young as eight years old. This, sadly, is not an isolated case as it has been seen in other parts of the country as well. Can a child or teenager who has been brainwashed into believing that they could trust no one apart from their abusers be blamed when they refuse to talk to the police, other authorities, charity workers or parents?

For me, cases of child exploitation – sexual or other-wise – have been the most harrowing of my career. As my knowledge and understanding has grown, I have reflected on cases and had to come to terms with what we might have missed.

Looking back in this way, with the benefit of hindsight and not being focused on finding solutions to the task in hand, stirs far more difficult emotions in me now than I ever experienced at the time. I often think about the suffering that was likely to have been occurring and I think to myself: *What more could I have done or what could I have done better?*

This is why I am so strident in my advocacy for approaches that involve persisting with talking to victims who seem uncooperative, or unwilling; delving into why they are behaving as they are, why they are going missing. The true power of these approaches, and the techniques used by dedicated and appropriately trained professionals, isn't just in the operational success they have. It's in the impact on the young people involved.

I attended one high-level strategic meeting about missing persons at the House of Commons, where the then minister for policing, Tim Loughton, was present. I was there alongside representatives of organisations who supported young people with a history of going missing and being in care and had brought some of their beneficiaries along to share their experiences.

Towards the end of the meeting, the minister spoke to one of the young people, a teenage boy, and said: 'Now, young man, I am the government minister in charge of this issue and have the power to make things change. What would you like me to change to make things better?'

The boy thought for a moment and then replied: 'Nothing. All I needed was for someone to keep on putting out their hand to help me. Even if I pushed it away and refused help, to keep on putting it there until I felt able to take that help.'

How profoundly important it is that we talk to victims, whatever age they are. That we listen, and that we keep on holding out our hands.

CHAPTER 11

International Borders

Has the person moved between two or more countries?

My work with Child Rescue Alert (CRA) had connected me to Netherlands-headquartered AMBER Alert Europe and its founder Frank Hoen. AMBER Alert Europe had primarily been set up to develop alert systems in European countries to engage the public in finding the most at-risk missing children.

Frank was building a system in the Netherlands alongside a criminal investigator, profiler and senior officer in the Dutch police called Carlo Schippers. Carlo was a long-time friend of mine whom I knew through the Global Missing Children's Network. I considered the system they had developed to be one of the most impressive and effective systems in Europe, if not the world, capable of alerting 12 million people within minutes.

If I was going to work with organisations to focus on missing children, *this* was the kind I wanted to be involved in. We had shared ambitions and I liked the way Frank did business. A product of the dot com boom, he was a true entrepreneur and getting the job done was what mattered, not endless hours of needless admin.

One day, while attending a meeting in Brussels, I confided in him about my new plans.

'Frank, I want out and am tired of the bureaucracy

here,' I said. 'If I left CEOP, would you give me some work as a consultant?'

Without missing a beat, Frank replied.

'Yes.'

It was all the encouragement I needed. A couple more conversations with other like-minded people in my network to secure further work followed. Before long I had a parachute, and I was ready to jump into the world of self-employment.

Resigning was far easier than I had expected. I did not realise just how stressed I had become in my role. All I had wanted to do for a long time was to try to improve the response to missing persons, but I was finding the bureaucracy too burdensome to bear any longer.

Charlie Hedges Advisory, the consultancy business that I established in January 2015 as a sole trader, became my freedom. Here I could earn a living while focusing on the issues that really mattered to me. I suppose I could have retired, but I still had the passion and energy for the cause. As long as I felt like I was able to make a difference, I decided I would carry on.

It was just the start of a rather incredible year for me. In April 2015, Shelley and I got married, with her two sons, Matt and Jon, becoming part of the family. The wedding was an intimate affair surrounded by a small group of our closest friends and family. We learned later that our registrar was the very same registrar who had married Prince Charles and Camilla, exactly ten years to the day!

We enjoyed a wonderful reception at The Manor at the Odney Club, which was owned by the John Lewis Partnership in Berkshire, Shelley's employer of more than thirty years. We were able to enjoy the venue's extensive grounds, thanks to the glorious sunshine and absence of any April showers. As we enjoyed drinks on the terrace, some of our guests even started an impromptu football match in their suits on a nearby grassed area, which typified the informality of the occasion. It was exactly what we had both wanted and the celebrations continued late into the evening, when our last guests retired to bed.

The momentous events didn't stop there, though. Not long after the wedding, I received a letter from the prime minister's office marked 'In Confidence'.

Whatever could this be? I thought, as I carefully opened the envelope and unfolded the letter.

As my eyes scanned the text, my heart skipped a beat.

I had been recommended to be appointed a Member of the British Empire in the Queen's Birthday Honours List 2015. The letter was in the strictest confidence and, subject to my accepting the honour, it would be published in some newspapers later in the year. To be recognised for my work in missing persons in this way was an incredible honour.

Among many other things, Frank and I shared a deep understanding of just how easy it was for people to cross international borders in Europe. We also recognised how widely exploited this was by criminals.

In my role as consultant to AMBER Alert Europe, I was to advise on matters relating to my police experience and also in relation to developing AMBER Alerts in other countries.

But Frank was also driven to try to achieve greater inter-operability of alerts and cross-border cooperation, which was something that chimed with my aims in relation to the police network and missing persons.

Working on the Ashya King case a year or so earlier, as I'd attempted to smooth the way for what I knew was going to be a complex operation, I had recognised the need for a network of missing person experts to tap into. Other formal networks for international cooperation and investigations existed, and I had no desire to undermine or bypass them, but I was convinced of the need to be able to easily contact missing person experts from other countries.

These thoughts were supported by extensive US research, backed by UK findings, showing that when a child was abducted and killed, in 76 per cent of the cases the child was killed within three hours after the abduction. Also, not forgetting the constant importance of the 'golden hour'.

'Frank,' I said. 'We need to build a network of police experts across Europe who can collaborate on cases and share good practice.'

'Yes, I agree,' he replied.

It was an idea that we had discussed from the outset of my consultancy role and was included in the tasks listed in my contract, but now building a network relating to missing children, transforming it into a recognised entity and acting as its coordinator became my primary goal.

I wanted there to be a missing persons expert in every country, making it possible to exchange good practices and learning between countries, and to be able to 'phone a friend' and talk through the issues when a difficult cross-border case arose. This was in no way intended to undermine or ignore the legal conventions that were required to enable cross-border cooperation, but rather to make them easier to implement and jointly work towards a successful outcome for the missing child.

'OK, great,' Frank said, after I had explained my idea at length. 'But what is your elevator pitch, Charlie?'

'What do you mean?' I asked, puzzled.

Frank and I did not always agree, especially with our different backgrounds, and we would sometimes argue strongly against each other, but it was a healthy way to develop new ideas and I benefitted greatly from his constructive challenges to my ideas and approaches.

'If you have an idea you want to develop and end up in an elevator with the person who can make it happen,' Frank explained, 'what are you going to say to convince them before they get out?'

It was an excellent question and it helped me to distil my thoughts into something that the right person could immediately buy into. In the end, it came down to this:

Borders across Europe are open, and that doesn't stop the bad guys from taking vulnerable children. We need to put something in place to stop that and we need a police network in place to support it.

And with that, the Police Expert Network was born.

I quickly settled into my new working life. Working between home and occasional visits to the AMBER Alert Europe offices in Beek, near Maastricht, the atmosphere and style of working was very different from what I was used to in law enforcement. It was far more relaxed, with less administration, but the whole team was extremely driven to achieve our collective objectives.

With carte blanche to develop my idea for the expert network, I set to it, alongside my wider work for the organisation. I had thought that my international travel had been extensive over the preceding years, but it now rose to new heights.

In my first year with AMBER Alert, I had twenty trips abroad in ten different countries for meetings, conferences and to build the network. This was all alongside other projects I was working on for my advisory, and a role as visiting lecturer at the University of Portsmouth, delivering lectures to students on human trafficking and child abduction.

To achieve Frank's ambition of greater interoperability of alerts, we took on the vast challenge of assisting countries who wanted to build their own AMBER Alert systems, starting with Slovakia.

There were lengthy meetings and discussions to develop the system and make it ready for use, with some of our team members advising on technical issues and how they should operate, and others engaging with local media organisations in the country. My role was mainly to liaise with the country's police, advising on procedures that they needed and training officers in how and when to use the system. We also worked with senior police officers and government officials to make sure that as many people in the country as possible were aware of what we were developing and supporting the final launch of the system once everything was in place.

After Slovakia, work with Luxembourg and Malta followed, which meant that there were four countries using our AMBER Alert system. Several other countries had their own systems and we liaised with them, learning from their good practices, and sharing those from other countries. There were new challenges to be faced in each territory, but the more countries that were using the same system for missing alerts, the greater the opportunity for improved cooperation when cross-border cases arose.

But it was not an easy task. Around the time I had started working with CRA, I had also worked on a project called LADS.eu with France and Belgium, regarding interoperability of alerts relating to cross-border child abductions. After many hours of debate and consultation including other countries in Europe, we eventually agreed upon a document of best practice published by the Council of the European Union.

Another organisation that we were closely involved in working with was FRONTEX, the EU borders agency. I became a frequent visitor to their headquarters in Warsaw, Poland. One project I was asked to join as part of this work was called VEGA children, which operated in a host of different countries to identify vulnerable children passing through the airports and ensure their safety.

I spent two weeks in Romania, working airside at Bucharest Airport with border guards from several countries to monitor passengers on arriving and departing flights. The experience provided a completely different perspective from policing and gave me a fascinating insight into parental abductions and the process they had in place in the country.

If one parent wanted to take the child out of the country, even for perfectly legitimate reasons, they still had to go through a process of registration and consent from the non-travelling parent or guardian.

On the surface, it made perfect sense and brought huge benefits from a child protection perspective. After all, if a parent was travelling with a child without any ill intentions or anything to hide, why would they not follow the process?

But the logistics of managing it were quite challenging. Despite being in place for around a decade, people were still turning up at the airport to go on holiday without having completed the process.

Observing and working closely with international border security teams also brought the emerging use of biometrics to my attention. I became a member of the Biometrics Institute where I reconnected with Professor Dame Sue Black, Baroness of Strome, a world-renowned forensic anthropologist. Throughout her career she had championed her belief that everyone deserved an identity and fought tirelessly for this in relation to unidentified bodies. Our paths had crossed previously in relation to child protection, but a new project we soon found ourselves working on together was more controversial in nature.

We were asked to establish a working group within the Institute to consider how biometrics could be of benefit in identifying missing children, looking at facial recognition technology. There was an opportunity to use the tech to identify children when they might be at risk, but it was fraught with a host of challenges around the issue of human rights and data protection. Over the course of many meetings, it became clear that there was a delicate balance between the use of this technology and protecting human rights, which made drawing definitive conclusions about its usefulness and potential for practical implementation difficult. In the end, it was too politically sensitive to lead to a specific outcome, but our conversations added important considerations to the wider debate about the technology's use.

Working with international agencies, being front line with border forces and exploring new technology all brought into sharp focus the challenges of working across borders; the importance of great ideas being properly implemented, the challenges of identifying suspicious behaviour among such large numbers of people and the pressure to move them through the border checks as quickly as possible, and also the appropriate and effective use of emerging technologies.

The insights were incredibly valuable when I later joined a team of specialists working on the development of a child protection course and accompanying manual for border guards in all EU countries. Once again, we came up against the challenges of writing something that would transcend differences in language, culture, tradition, law and local procedures. Knowing the basic principles is one thing, but being able to describe them in a way that was easily implemented was something else.

Six months after receiving my letter of invitation from the prime minister's office, I attended Windsor Castle to be presented with my MBE. Shelley, my sister Sue and her partner Bill came with me as my guests. As we drove up Long Walk, with the castle at the top of the rise, we were struck by the grandeur of the occasion. We were directed where to park the car by a police officer.

'Good morning. Wonderful occasion. Congratulations,' were his opening words.

'You will notice the Royal Standard flag,' he continued. 'That indicates Her Majesty is in residence and will be presenting the honours today.'

Every official treated us with the same courtesy and made us feel so special. We walked the rest of the way to the castle, with staff in their formal dress and uniforms.

The guests were taken to the spectacular Waterloo Chamber, to the sound of the Countess of Wessex's String Orchestra playing in the gallery, where the ceremony would take place, while I and other recipients were taken to an adjoining room for a briefing.

As we were left to have a drink and mingle, I struck up a conversation with the TV presenter, journalist, historian and horticulturist, Wesley Kerr, who was also to receive an MBE for his services to heritage.

'I notice that you are the only person here wearing brown shoes,' he said with a huge smile. 'Do you think that is allowed, or is there a strict dress code for black shoes?'

I looked down at my feet and laughed. To be quite honest, I hadn't even considered the colour of my shoes.

'That may be the case,' I said. 'But I didn't get here by being one of the crowd.'

Highly amused by our interaction, we continued to chat about our respective work until it was time for the ceremony. Lined up in the Waterloo Chamber and waiting for my turn, I found myself in a lively conversation with the deputy head gardener from Wakehurst Garden, part of Kew Gardens, until suddenly . . .

'Excuse me, sirs,' came a sharp voice.

It was one of the attendants, staring sternly at us. We were clearly the naughty boys at the back making too much noise! Fortunately, I wasn't able to get into too much more trouble as I was next in line.

As my name was announced, I walked towards Her Majesty, as I had been briefed to do.

Charles Hedges, for services to the National Crime Agency.

As I stood in front of the Queen, who was not in full regalia but wearing an elegant purple dress and some jewellery, I gave a respectful smile as she started a conversation around my work for the NCA.

'Thank you, Your Majesty,' I said. 'The main focus of my work is missing children.'

'Oh, is that a problem?' she asked.

If there was ever a time for one of Frank's beloved elevator pitches, it was now. I seized my moment.

'Yes, the latest data tells us that the police took in excess of 300,000 calls in relation to missing persons, the majority of which relate to missing children,' I said. 'Many of these are repeat incidences of going missing and each incident is an indication of something that is wrong in that child's life, including abuse and exploitation.'

As I spoke the Queen's eyebrows raised, and I hoped that I had conveyed the information in a suitable manner. But I was never going to miss an opportunity to raise awareness at such high levels of power.

As her expression returned to normal, she acknowledged the information, congratulated me on my work and I went on my way.

It was a brief but extremely special moment. I would have loved my parents to have known about how far I'd come and seen me standing there. When they passed away within months of one another in 2004, I had been so early in my journey in missing persons. So much had happened since. But I knew that they would have been proud, not just of my achievements, but the fact that I was doing something I loved and that had real purpose.

After the formalities were over, I met up with Shelley, Sue and Bill and we took a tour of the castle, then it was time to leave. Before we did, I spotted Wesley again.

'Ah, you got away with it then,' he said, gesturing at my shoes. 'You didn't get taken off to the Tower!'

'It seems that way,' I laughed.

As we were making our way out of the building, Shelley smiled at me.

'Did you recognise the piece the orchestra were playing as you went up to meet the Queen?' she asked.

'Yes,' I replied. '"Ave Maria". The same as you walked in to when we were married.'

It was a wonderful coincidence and made the experience even more memorable. We were all staggered by how special the occasion was, how delightful all the staff were and that we never felt rushed. We took the opportunity to embrace the moment and take it all in.

As my work with AMBER Alert continued, a dynamic emerged between Frank and me, with him leading lobbying campaigns to gain support for our work, getting the attention of various police forces, governments and agencies. With that job done, I would find myself being launched into the thick of it as AMBER Alert's resident missing persons expert.

Every meeting I attended, every project I participated in, every country we launched the alert system in and every conference I spoke at was a chance to add a new expert to my network.

I used the organisation's profile and reputation to encourage new countries to join, to share good practices and exchange information about missing children. As I built a robust network, we were also working hard in Brussels to gain political support.

This was mainly led by Frank, supported by me, speaking at various meetings within the European Parliament. This intensive lobbying led to us gaining the support for our initiatives by 465 Members of the European Parliament from all EU Member States signing a written declaration in 2016 supporting it.

It was the greatest level of support given to an initiative by Members of the European Parliament since 2011 – an astonishing and a huge achievement. But it didn't mean the passage was going to be an easy one; it was simply a significant positive first step.

Despite having similar objectives, there was often a divergence of views among the various organisations and NGOs about how things should be done. One of the other large organisations in Europe that worked in our field was Missing Children Europe and, over the years, sometimes relations were supportive and cordial and at other times less so. Also, despite the huge support from elected members of the EU, our work was held back by its officials.

It was frustrating, of course, but we were so sure of what we were doing that we continued to drive the agenda forward, exploring options for a central focus for the network.

We continued to grow the membership of the network, but it needed an online presence to make it widely accessible, and to have a place in an official law enforcement organisation. After exploratory meetings with several different organisations, we found a potential solution.

We believed that the network should be housed within the law enforcement agency of the European Union, the European Union Agency for Law Enforcement Cooperation, which was known as Europol.

But there was one major obstacle. Missing children was outside of their remit.

The criteria for its work were organised crime that involved two or more European countries. Their officially quoted terms of reference were: *'Europol exists to support and strengthen action and cooperation by Member States' police authorities and other law enforcement services in preventing and combating serious crime. This includes crimes affecting two or more Member States, terrorism and forms of crime which affect a common interest covered by an EU policy.'*

A missing child that had crossed from one country to another ticked one box, but if the movement did not involve serious crime, then it was outside of their scope, and would be left to law enforcement in the involved countries to deal with alone.

'But going missing is an indicator of something happening in a child's life,' I said to Frank. 'We need to convince them that a missing child is sometimes an indicator of organised crime.'

While working with AMBER Alert Europe we were aware of extremely high levels of migration and the associated concerns about unaccompanied minors. I had always believed this to be a major issue relating to missing children, with children travelling across Europe and simply disappearing.

Monitoring systems at international borders were not able to cope, and it was not known where many children went, making them vulnerable to exploitation and abuse, the scale of which I didn't believe we really knew.

What we did know, however, was that organised crime groups had certainly seen migration as an opportunity, leveraging other people's distress and unhappiness to make huge amounts of money.

Some of this was seen in people trafficking, where the criminals take control of vulnerable people and – often based on false promises – exploit them and then sell them to other exploiters. The profits of worldwide human trafficking were estimated to be a staggering $150 billion per year.

In other cases, people smugglers are involved. There was a subtle distinction between the two. Trafficking people was carried out through force, fear, fraud and so on, and was not something people would knowingly consent to.

Smuggling was done with the person's consent. They wished for a better life elsewhere and were willing to pay someone to get them there, usually in the region of £2,000 to £10,000. However, we observed that what started out as consensual often turned bad when those involved were taken advantage of. Once in the system, they were at the mercy of the smugglers who would often demand additional money or gain control of the people by assaulting and raping them.

Combined with what I had observed throughout my career, with missing always being an indicator of some other issue or harm, I believed this was enough to justify its inclusion in Europol.

We attended several discussions at Europol headquarters in The Hague to present our rationale, citing examples of human trafficking, child exploitation and abduction where being missing had indeed been an indicator of serious and organised criminal activity.

Eventually our argument was accepted, and it was agreed that our network would be supported by Europol and that the organisation would host it on the European Platform of Experts (EPE), which already housed many Europe-wide policing expert groups.

There was still much work to be done to get the network to be officially recognised by the EU, but it was a huge step forward and almost unheard of for an NGO to achieve.

One ongoing challenge was that the organisation behind such networks was usually an official law enforcement or similar body, due to concerns about an external group being privy to sensitive information. There had to be a clear divide between a non-police organisation and any confidential matters that might be discussed by members.

To navigate this, we agreed there should be a rotating presidency by one of the member countries. AMBER Alert would provide the secretariat and continue to develop and manage the network, leaving the law enforcement bodies to get on with their work. The network became known as the Police Expert Network on Missing Persons (PEN-MP), and its remit expanded from just missing children to also include missing adults.

I knew from my own personal experience that the network would become a vital tool. There were many times I would have been able to act more swiftly and coherently if it had been in place, allowing cases to be resolved more quickly and efficiently, so our drive for official recognition by the EU continued.

Our involvement with international governments and law enforcement agencies, and AMBER Alert Europe's growing profile, also allowed us to drive many other vital changes to improve the response to issues related to missing persons.

One such initiative that we advocated was a Common European Approach on Missing Children and Missing Persons, which was established around four pillars.

1. Missing Persons Risk Triage for immediate risk identification of a missing child
2. Enhanced cross-border law enforcement cooperation on missing children
3. Connecting the public with law enforcement in the search for a missing child

4. Preventing children from going missing as a joint effort of all stakeholders

The 'Missing Persons Risk Triage' was based on both Frank's and my deep understanding of the value and importance of understanding risk, something I had raised even in my earliest work.

The title 'Risk Triage' drew a comparison to triage in medical situations, where the urgency of response is determined. 'Triage' had originated during the Napoleonic wars when the large numbers of casualties demanded a system to deal with the most severe first. With the large number of missing person cases, a similar system was needed. The approach highlighted the need for a definitive guide on the matter, and I agreed to use my expertise to write it.

The guide explained how to assess risk and went through a series of questions that should be posed when approaching a missing person case, explaining what each meant. Fundamental to the guide was encouraging investigators, police and practitioners to assess both the missing person's personal circumstances and the environment to which they are exposed – the two combined indicated how significant the risk was.

Risk factors had been identified over the years and used as indicators to guide decision-makers in planning their investigation.

However, those decision-makers were given little or no training in this type of risk assessment. Without proper training, how could they be expected to know what the many factors meant, and how they should be interpreted?

The guide led to a training programme being developed which I went on to deliver in countries across Europe,

South America and Jamaica. In those places, we found that many of the processes that were standard in the UK, US and Australia, which were considered leaders in the development of missing person procedures, were not so well developed or in some cases did not exist at all. There was also a limited understanding of what missing really meant, and its status as an indicator. Through our training we were trying to spread the word and improve processes wherever we could.

Operating as Charlie Hedges Advisory not only saw me implementing my experience dealing with international cases in countries around the world, but it also allowed me to work with international organisations to bring their approaches to the UK.

I had met Andy McCullough earlier in my career. He worked for the charity Railway Children, which was based in the UK, India and East Africa, and worked with children who went missing and came to harm on the streets.

In the 25 years that the charity had been in operation, it had reached more than 275,000 children in the territories that it worked in, tackling the same challenges that I had frequently faced, where the existence of abuse and exploitation was not accepted, understood or – at its very worst – was denied.

I felt a great synergy with its mission to 'fight to change the story' of such children and its pioneering work to 'get to street children before the streets get to them', so when Andy asked me to join a new project known as the Transport and Communities Awareness Programme, I was eager to join the team and lead the project.

Andy and I were very different. I was the more conventional product of a disciplined organisation, following convention and dress codes, usually a suit. Andy did not follow any conventions, had more tattoos and piercings than you could count and, whatever the meeting or environment, would never change his dress style from jeans and a T-shirt. So markedly different were our backgrounds and appearance that I would sometimes ironically refer to us as 'the twins'.

Despite our differences, we made a good team. Andy's compassion, based on lived experience of knowing what it was like to be in some of the situations that missing children found themselves, brought something very special to our work and I knew that together we'd be able to make a difference.

Andy asked me to review existing child safeguarding procedures and identify opportunities for further development around the rail transport network in the UK, working principally with Network Rail, train operating companies, British Transport Police and Transport for London.

We recognised that vulnerable people frequented the transport infrastructure not just for transport, but also for shelter and safety, and agreed that whatever emerged from my review should be a best response that was applicable initially to just children but eventually changed to an approach to all ages.

Railway stations, especially those in large urban areas, had large numbers of people working there in a variety of capacities, so my idea was to create a community-based approach, connecting everyone who worked in stations and giving them an awareness of safeguarding issues.

The project highlighted how to identify vulnerable persons and how to respond to them. Apart from the train and station staff, this needed to incorporate anyone who worked in retail outlets, cafes, as cleaners or in any other role at the station. The more people that were on the lookout, the better, and it would also allow them to support each other when needed, giving benefits far wider than our project scope.

One rail worker shared a story of when he was working on a train travelling into London late in the evening and encountered a young man whom he was concerned about.

'It wasn't anything specific,' he said. 'His manner and demeanour were just "off". When I asked if he was OK, he said he was. But something just didn't feel right.'

He trusted his instinct and decided to follow him at a discreet distance when he got off the train. Luckily, there was an officer at the terminus whom he asked to speak to the young man.

'The officer was also concerned after speaking to him,' he explained. 'Eventually, the young man told the officer that he had run away from home and was nervous about what he was going to do now that he was in London.'

From there, the police were able to ensure the young man's safety. It was an inspirational story and a credit to the rail worker who had acted on his concerns. It was also valuable evidence to support our project, and just the sort of action that we wanted to encourage through the safeguarding training.

The final product included the provision of training in vulnerabilities, how to identify them and what to do. Crucially, it did not require every person to give a full safeguarding response, but instead connect them with the person they were worried about, allow them to show concern, provide reassurance and know whom to contact for assistance. Each location had one or more programme 'champions' who would promote what we were doing and be trained in delivering awareness sessions to other members of staff in a cascade system.

Over a period of about twenty months, I delivered training to champions at railway stations across the UK. We also pulled in staff from London Underground and the bus operating companies that operated buses at railway stations, ensuring that more people were aware of how to identify vulnerable people and how to help them.

PEN-MP was finally officially recognised by the EU on 18 October 2019. On this date, all European Member States supported the formalisation of the first and only police network that brings together law enforcement specialists on missing persons, and missing children specifically. The travelling and engagement undertaken over the course of four years by AMBER Alert Europe resulted in a membership of more than eighty law enforcement experts from thirty-four EU and non-EU countries. It was an incredible achievement.

As well as establishing PEN-MP and implementing AMBER Alert in many new countries, Frank and I also lobbied for preventive alerts being included in the Schengen Information System (SIS), the most widely used and largest information sharing system for security and border management in Europe.

These alerts were designed to protect certain categories of vulnerable persons, including children at risk of being abducted by their own parents, relatives or guardians, and vulnerable persons whose travel must be prevented, unless they have the necessary authorisations, as they are at risk of being taken unlawfully abroad. Both have been legally adopted by the EU.

Measures such as these are always underpinned by continued training and sharing of good practices and approaches learned from experts from different organisations and different countries.

With this in mind, I took on further work with the International Centre for Missing & Exploited Children (ICMEC), working for Caroline Humer, another long-time friend who had worked at ICMEC for several years. I was developing policies and procedures relating to different aspects of missing children procedures, including the Photo Distribution Framework, The Emergency Child Alert System Framework and The Child Alert Framework and a photo dissemination strategy for Ecuador.

As part of a travelling team of international experts for ICMEC, my focus was training on four topics: Family Advocacy, Search, Preventing Runaways and Missing from Care, and Media, Social Media and Missing Children.

In many aspects, the UK has developed much further than other places with a more detailed and effective response to missing persons cases, and probably more research carried out here than in other countries.

There have been many times over the years when reading policies and procedures from other places that I have thought *Oh, this sounds familiar,* only to realise that parts are copies of my words, published in an array of documents.

They say imitation is the best form of flattery and I am always delighted when people copy what I write. For me it validates that which I have fought so many years for, and the fact that these documents provide guidance that will ultimately help some of the world's most vulnerable people gives me great satisfaction.

However, although the UK has made great strides in this area, that is not to say that we get it right all the time, and we still have much to learn. Many of the issues that emerged from my work with Professor Dame Sue Black, Baroness of Strome and the Institute of Biometrics have still not been resolved, but as the world moves further forward in its relationship with technology, our response and approaches continue to develop and evolve. There is now more use being made of facial recognition, especially in relation to counter-terrorism, but challenges in its implementation elsewhere remain.

The issue of the missing also never remains static; our world and the environments we inhabit are always changing, the tools and networks we have access to shift over time and our policies and procedures need to keep pace with these changes.

Take Brexit, for example. After the vote to leave the EU was confirmed, the UK's access to the Schengen Information System was limited, and in 2021 revoked completely. As of 2023 the process for the UK gaining access to EU data sets was stated to be at 'a very early stage' and not expected to be completed before 2027/28.

Also, in 2022, it was announced that the PEN-MP should be open only to police members and that AMBER Alert Europe would step aside from its secretariat role. I did not agree with this decision as experience has taught me that only organisations like AMBER Alert Europe had the time and the determination to take forward the large amount of work that was required to make such a network survive and succeed.

I hope I am wrong, and that it continues to thrive, but time will tell.

It is changes such as these – and many more varied ones relating to political, social and economic issues – that inevitably pose new questions and challenges for those of us working in the missing, and we have to respond to those accordingly.

CHAPTER 12

Cold Case

What happens to those left behind?

Having now spent more than twenty years working with the families of the missing on both new and active cases and long-term unsolved or 'cold' cases, I have become increasingly and acutely aware of the impact that going missing had on those who were left behind – the parents, siblings, extended family, friends and colleagues of those who disappeared.

One such long-term unsolved case that had occupied the public's mind for more than a decade was that of three-year-old Madeleine McCann, who went missing on the evening of 3 May 2007 from an apartment in Praia da Luz, Portugal. It was a case that has commanded so much attention over the years that I'd be amazed to find someone who has not heard of it.

Madeleine, or 'Maddie' as she was known to her family, was on holiday with her parents, Kate and Gerry McCann, her two-year-old twin siblings, a group of family friends and their children when she vanished as her parents dined in a restaurant just 180ft away from their apartment.

At the time of her disappearance, I wasn't working in the operational side of missing persons but in the years that followed, I met both Kate and Gerry on several occasions.

The first time was about a year after Maddie's disappearance when I was working at the Missing Persons Bureau, and they had been invited to speak at a conference. The decision was somewhat controversial at the time as the investigation was still ongoing and the couple's *arguido* or 'suspect' status with the Portuguese police had only recently been lifted.

As it was an event for police officers involved in missing person cases, that controversy was well managed, and it was useful to hear their perspective. We also understood the process that the Portuguese police were following. Statistics told us that stranger abductions were extremely rare, with the majority resulting from the actions of someone known to the victim. That said, statistics did not guarantee to predict the outcome; they were a guide that provided a useful context, and each case had to be considered on its own unique circumstances.

Bearing in mind the higher statistical likelihood of someone known to the victim being the perpetrator, difficult questions had to be asked, and decisions made. As unpleasant and upsetting as it was for the family, from a policing perspective I understood that it was essential to the investigation to question Maddie's parents and friends, examine their movements and consider if it was possible for them to have been involved in her disappearance.

Ruling them out would allow other scenarios to be considered and investigated, and remove any lingering doubt, particularly given the high media profile of the case.

Our paths also crossed when I began working on Child Rescue Alert (CRA) as both Kate and Gerry were interested in the work we were doing, having already launched a campaign calling for a Europe-wide missing child alert system similar to AMBER Alert in the US.

They believed that had such a system been in place, the chances of recovering Maddie would have been greater. Gerry and Kate highlighted how police needed as much cooperation as possible, and they were convinced that EU countries would be able to work together to set up a rapid response network, preventing other families from enduring the pain that they had.

At that time, just one year into the case, they still had great hope that Maddie would be found. By 2011 the Metropolitan Police had announced the launch of 'Operation Grange', in which it would bring its expertise to Maddie's case at the request of the then Home Secretary Theresa May. Its role would be to review all previous investigations of the case and explore any new leads.

But six years later, in 2017, her whereabouts were still unknown. I had, over the years, received information from people who claimed to know where she was or what had happened to her. People would contact me to say that they knew where she had been buried, that she was living in another country and a whole host of other explanations as to what had happened.

Some said that they knew this because they were psychics or mediums, others that they had heard it from somewhere or someone else. Regardless of my opinions on the sources, or how likely I felt the information was to be accurate or useful, I passed it all on to officers at Operation Grange at New Scotland Yard, the official investigators, so they could consider it properly.

I had also been asked by the media for comment when there were developments to the case, or significant anniversaries. The most common question posed to me as a missing persons expert is always 'What do you think happened to Madeleine McCann?' It is and was a difficult question to answer. At the time, without intimate knowledge of the facts of the case, it was something that I generally declined to answer as any response I gave would be pure speculation.

Maddie's case continued to endure in the public's imagination, a classic unsolved mystery. It gripped the public like a novel they were eager to turn the page on. They all wanted to know what happened.

Using information gleaned from media reports about Maddie's case, 'armchair detectives' came up with their theories and shared them online, sometimes finding their way back into the media, such was the demand for news on the topic. Every such theory of belief had to be assessed and evaluated by the police to determine if it had relevance to the investigation and took up enormous amounts of time.

The desire for answers about her disappearance meant that the case was believed to be one of the most heavily reported missing persons cases in modern history.

However, as the media circus ensued, I was always conscious that these were not fictional characters but real people who were really living this nightmare.

I knew how vital it was to maintain attention on a long-term missing person case, but to be of use it had to support an investigation strategy. As Maddie's case became a cultural phenomenon, the agenda for some quarters of the media changed.

It was no longer *just* about finding Maddie. It was about satisfying readers' interest, selling newspapers and generating clicks on websites by publishing sensational headlines and masterfully filleting what had actually been said, and using it out of context to make it seem like something else altogether had been said.

While I will not speculate on what happened, there are some important principles of investigation that are crucial to a case of this nature.

Understanding the risk to determine the urgency of the response: it cannot be anything but high risk when a child of this age disappears at that time of night, until the disappearance has been explained and an innocent reason found.

Clearing the ground under your feet: whether it be by searching or enquiry, all of the immediate and obvious matters must be resolved and the area close to the disappearance searched.

Considering experience and research data: these tell us that someone close to the missing person is most likely to be involved and they must be ruled in or ruled out of having any involvement. This does not imply that Maddie's parents were responsible, but this is the elephant in the room and must be addressed as soon as possible.

Preserving evidence: as once this is lost or contaminated it cannot be regained.

These are just the starting points and solid foundations. If these are laid, then the ongoing investigation will be sound.

Observing how missing persons cases were managed and publicised, seeing what worked and what didn't, always set me off thinking how things could be improved. I was always seeking new information and techniques and considering how they might be applied practically.

While attending an international conference on 'missing' issues at Abertay University in Dundee in the summer of 2017, I was surprised by just how much research had been carried out and was ongoing in the two years since the last conference.

It was such a useful and comprehensive update on the latest statistics, techniques and learnings from around the world. But why had it taken so long for me, a missing persons expert, to hear about it?

It struck me as being inefficient and wasteful and one of those things that could, perhaps, be managed better.

As with many conferences focused on the missing, I

also benefitted from speaking to people from very different backgrounds, but with a shared passion for the issue. One of these was Tanja Conway-Grim, who was attending with Cranfield University.

Cranfield was somewhere I'd been looking to link to, owing to its renowned forensics department. When I spotted Tanja sporting a university-branded polo shirt, I seized the opportunity.

Tanja was undertaking her Master of Research (MRes) in Forensics but had become involved in the subject of the missing from a place of lived experience. She first went missing in 1966 as a toddler and has had missing episodes throughout her life for a variety of reasons. She had also recently been diagnosed as being on the autistic spectrum.[24]

Where my experience came solely from my work as a professional, Tanja brought the perspective of having been a missing person, a carer for a missing person/person at risk of going missing, of working with county lines missing young people, not to mention practical and research experience in the field.

Over the years, I had learned how important it was to understand the perspectives of those with lived experience – something well outside of my own life and another lesson learned about looking at an issue from all sides.

Her perspective as someone with autism was also incredibly valuable, providing insight that fed into both my professional and personal lives. When Shelley and I had first moved in together, both of her sons – Matt and Jon – were quite young. Jon, the younger of the two, struggled with concepts and was quite hard to communicate with, often not

24 www.locate.international/about/tanja-conway-grim/

responding to situations in the way we expected. It was challenging at times, and we spoke to numerous consultants to try and establish if Jon was on the autistic spectrum. It emerged that he was not, but that he did have a sensory processing disorder and dyspraxia, which affects his coordination.

This did not mean that he had an illness or disease, it just meant that his brain worked in a different way to other people.

As one consultant wonderfully put it: 'He has a wiring diagram that is different to other people.'

Learning about how Jon saw the world, and now speaking to Tanja about her experiences, was immensely educational for me, and it resonated with my work in trying to understand missing persons with such vulnerabilities and what makes them disappear.

We were also able to discuss some of the challenges faced by people who had gone missing and returned, particularly those who had gone missing as children or young people, and the impact later in life.

One such challenge was the right to be forgotten. Before the explosion in online and social media, appeals to find a missing person would be delivered through print media, radio and TV. Old content could not be readily searched and accessed by the public, making the publicity relatively transient and much harder to find after the media appeals had stopped.

But digital media had changed that landscape, so that missing person reports might be findable forever. It was something of a paradox, an extremely useful but also potentially dangerous means of sharing information about what is happening in a person's life, that could be damaging to the individual.

I personally knew of instances where a person who had been missing had applied for a job, and their potential employer had found reports they had been missing as a child online, raising difficult questions and causing embarrassment.

Not to mention the discrimination that such information might provoke.

It was something Frank and I had considered deeply at AMBER Alert Europe, recognising that we had to be careful about what is said during an appeal and remembering that every individual had the right to be forgotten in that context.

Like me, Tanja was also passionate about those left behind – the parents, children, friends and other loved ones, including those involved in long-term 'cold cases' where there was no active police investigation.

Ending up on the same train back to Edinburgh after the conference, we continued debating the many issues surrounding the missing and the information that was available.

'It strikes me that there should be somewhere anyone can access all the latest information on the missing,' I said. 'We shouldn't need to wait two years for the next conference to find it.'

I knew this was the kind of project that would benefit enormously from my consultative approach. I wanted as many different voices and perspectives involved as possible. Police, voluntary sector, search, lived experience . . .

Tanja was exactly the kind of voice we'd need involved.

We'd already established that we were very much on the same page, so I figured it was worth asking. Once again, I seized the opportunity.

'Will you work with me on this?' I asked. Tanja pondered the offer for a moment.

'I'd be happy to be involved,' she said. 'But is it just about the police? Who else would benefit from this?'

It was exactly the kind of question I wanted to hear. Delivered from a place of deep knowledge and understanding. With the right people in the room, we could make this idea into something that could be of enormous use and value.

After we went our separate ways on arrival in Edinburgh, I began to formulate a plan for a centre just like the one we had discussed. Tanja's initial questions had already broadened my initial scope, and our discussion had prompted a flood of questions.

What would it contain? What would it offer and to whom? What would its purpose be?

To my mind, it needed to house the latest information, research and guidance, and it was an opportunity to have a place to collate good practices from around the world, but it could also offer other services, such as training.

There were challenges to think through as well. Would this centre be NGO, charity or a formal police-backed organisation? Would it be physical or virtual? Would it be possible to get funding?

And what about cold cases?

Tanja and I had discussed how there were thousands of unsolved missing person cases in the UK alone. Some dated back decades when processes and technology were far less advanced. Could something be done to draw attention to those, perhaps resolve them and bring closure to those who had been left behind? One such case that had significantly affected me predated even my own first major missing person case.

It was the case of Damien Nettles, the sixteen-year-old boy who disappeared from Cowes on the Isle of Wight during a night out with a friend. He had vanished on 2 November 1996, around a year before I found the note on my desk about Rob's case.

I had always been aware of Damien's story. While I was investigating Rob's disappearance, I had recognised the similarities in attitudes among police towards both Rob and Damien's cases.

He's a young lad off having fun. He'll turn up.

But Damien never did.

It was nearly twenty years into my career in the missing before I met Damien's mother, Val Nettles. In 2016, she launched a campaign for 'Damien's Law', and a mutual acquaintance had introduced us as they thought I might be able to usefully advise Val on what she was trying to achieve.

She was calling on the prime minister to introduce a law where missing young male cases were treated equally to young girls, and asking for a number of changes to be made to the Association of Chief Police Officers (ACPO) Manual of Guidance.

Damien's case was another example of where the police did not immediately recognise its seriousness and the 'golden hour' was missed. Had they acted faster, I believed potentially more could have been done.

Speaking to Val, she told me of the difficulty she and her family had experienced while trying to engage with the police, both in the early stages of the investigation and in the many years that followed.

Much like Rob's mum, Val was not properly listened to. There had been a lack of urgency and no consistency in communication with the family. But unlike Rob's case, despite many hypotheses and lines of enquiry, there had never been any resolution.

Val spoke of her experience of 'ambiguous loss', a term coined by Dr Pauline Boss in the 1970s to describe loss that isn't clear. The family had long suspected foul play and there had been investigations following such lines of enquiry, with eight arrests for conspiracy to murder, but no charges were ever brought. With no confirmed account of what had happened to Damien, no body to bury, the family were left in limbo, unsure if they even *should* mourn.

Losing someone dear to you is obviously always traumatic, be it a separation, a death that might be expected through old age or long-term illness, an unexpected death like an accident or sudden illness, or sometimes horrible reasons such as being the victim of a crime. All of these experiences are devastating, but there is at least an explanation for what happened.

Ambiguous loss is different, and it is the state that people with a missing loved one often find themselves in. The closure that you would usually experience with loss is simply not available. Those who live with ambiguous loss are unable to grieve, unable to move on, and always hoping that the missing person will walk back through the door.

There really isn't a more agonising state to be in.

Damien's family were not alone in the experience, either. Over the years, I had met the families of long-term missing persons whose lives were fixed to a timetable set in the time that the person was last seen. They could not bring themselves to throw their possessions away, redecorate their bedroom or move house. Every birthday, Christmas or other memorable date was marked by hope that there would be no more such dates without the person, and that they would come home.

I met one family who preserved their daughter's bedroom exactly as it was on the day that she disappeared twenty years earlier, because they felt that interfering with it would be wrong until they knew what had happened to her. Another family would not move house on the grounds that if their son did decide to come home, they would not be there when he arrived on the doorstep. It was something they were not willing to risk, no matter how slim the chances. There were also parents who still bought birthday and Christmas presents for their missing sons and daughters each year, so they would not be without a gift should they turn up.

It may appear strange, but it's not until you really understand the impact of someone you love going missing and there being no explanation that you really get to the heart of the matter.

These are just a few examples, but everyone was different. Some people said they had moved on but had not given up hope nor stopped making efforts to find their loved one.

But it wasn't just the emotional toll, it was the practical issues as well. If you did not know if a person was dead or alive, how should you deal with their financial, personal and business affairs?

I used my policing experience to advise Val on how best to tailor her requests for Damien's Law to make them implementable and possible to include in guidelines and frameworks. It wasn't that her ideas were wrong, they just needed shaping to fit into the way that policing operates.

As we had worked together, I'd realised that while missing persons was a challenging area for professionals like police and other statutory services to navigate, for the families of the missing it was all but impossible. There were so many questions they needed to think about.

What should you do if a loved one goes missing, and when?
What should happen after you report it to the police?
What can you do to help?

As ideas prompted by my discussions with Tanja started to circulate in my brain, the conversations I'd had with Val also sprang to the front of my mind. Everything pointed to the same solution.

A central hub of information about going missing . . .

In my gut, I recognised the familiar feeling of identifying a challenge that needed to be addressed, and I got to work.

I started to gather people who might be able to help us examine ideas about how a specialist centre for information on the missing might be created. For our first official meeting on the matter, Tanja, David 'Woody' Woodgate from Lowland Rescue and Dr Karl Harrison, a specialist in forensics, came together to discuss what might be possible.

We came up with a working project title, the 'Centre for Expertise on Missing Persons' and decided it would look at case reviews and cold cases, provide training and act as a central point where all information about missing persons could be found.

I began pouncing on relevant people at opportune moments to test out our ideas. Some official bodies and charities were suspicious about our motives, some were dismissive, and others held a variety of different views that I knew needed consideration.

After all, we couldn't just force the idea on people. We had to refine, develop and prove the need for it so others would be convinced it had a place going forward. I knew that could not happen overnight.

As our advisory group grew, I invited Val Nettles to join our project. We'd remained in regular contact and I could feel the pain that she still had, as well as her desire to turn her suffering into something positive for other families of the missing.

'There are thousands of us,' she said. 'We didn't know what to do at the start, and we're all struggling to cope with the aftermath alone, still not knowing what to do.'

'I promise I'll do what I can to change that,' I told her.

Talking to her about her experiences of losing Damien continually reinforced my thoughts about the difficulties of navigating the world of missing persons for someone new to it. The promise I'd made fitted my ideas for the new centre, providing publicly available resources demystifying the processes and improving access to support.

The idea of a central hub of information on missing issues also became one of the pillars of 'Damien's Law', as Val's own campaign continued.

It took time to navigate the complexities of creating something that would work practically and have the authority to solve problems. In fact, we were still working it out when the next international conference on 'missing' issues rolled around in 2019, this time taking place in Liverpool.

Our plan for the Centre for Expertise on Missing Persons still involved reviewing cases and investigating cold cases, but an encounter in Liverpool with an old contact from my days at the NCA changed that.

Former Detective Inspector Dave Grimstead had worked on several missing person investigations and, after he retired, had started to create a volunteer team to look at cold cases and unidentified bodies.

The scope of our project was so vast that I saw no point in going into unnecessary competition with Dave. It made far more sense for us to leave that part of the plan with him while we focused on the rest. As we chatted, we explored how to collaborate and develop our ideas and what the outcomes might look like.

'There is a huge gap in what is needed to look at cold cases and what the police can provide,' he said. 'They just don't have the resources. Let's keep in touch and see what we can do to support each other.'

With that agreed, I focused on other areas of the centre of expertise that I wanted to develop and decided that an online hub was the answer. It could bring all of that vital knowledge about missing persons together in one place and be available at the click of a button.

After all, what did most of us do when there was something we didn't know the answer to, or how to fix something? We googled it.

Although it might not be able to fix the problem, any member of the public who found themselves in the unfortunate and difficult circumstance of someone going missing would at least be able to find out what to do, and what to expect from the police and other authorities.

It would be a powerful tool and its creation was to be guided by a diverse and knowledgeable volunteer working group, comprising Val, Tanja and me, my old friend Geoff Newiss and representatives from the charity Missing People, National Police Chiefs Council, the NCA Missing Persons Unit, Professor Karen Shalev-Greene, who had led the development of the Centre for Missing Persons Studies at the University of Portsmouth where I lectured, and Dr Susan Giles from the University of Liverpool.

Our vision was to create a website that signposted to everything anyone might want to know about missing, but not provide any immediate or direct services. There were already plenty of organisations doing that and we wanted to elevate and promote them.

We wanted the website to be of use to anyone who was, had been or was contemplating going missing, together with anyone connected to them, like families, friends and colleagues. We wanted it to be a resource for police officers and other professionals, academics and anyone else with an interest in the subject.

Despite all the expertise in our group, none of it lay in building websites. Thankfully, we were ably assisted by Matt Sessions from the University of Central Lancashire and a student at the University of Manchester called Nic Fox, who gave hours of their time as volunteers.

To make it completely clear that this was a resource for everyone, we decided that naming it an 'expert' network might exclude or alienate some groups, and instead came up with a new name: The Missing Persons Information Hub (MPIH). There is no financial support for this project and everyone involved gave their time on a voluntary basis.

Thanks to Karen's involvement, the Centre for Missing Persons Studies at the University of Portsmouth decided to donate its extensive library of publications relating to all aspects of missing persons, replicating its wealth of knowledge online, and making it instantly accessible.

We added information about all aspects of missing; what it meant, where to get help, the processes surrounding it and explanations of key terms. As we built up the resources, which included many of the guidance documents I had authored over the years, I remembered my promise to Val regarding the difficulties faced by the families of the missing.

I promise I'll do what I can to change that, I'd told her.

Working in collaboration with Tanja, Val and Val's friend Caroline Lyons, who had long supported her search for Damien, I drafted a booklet titled *Guidance for Families & Friends: Advice on what to do if someone is missing.*

The simple yet comprehensive nineteen-page booklet explained what happens when someone goes missing, what concerned families and friends should do, and what response they should expect from the police, to equip them to be able to act appropriately and to challenge any failures in these processes.

True to my promise to Val, I also developed a two-page 'quick guide' that contained the points to consider immediately when someone went missing, so families could easily work out what steps needed to be taken in the all-important 'golden hour'.

Both of these documents can be accessed via MPIH.

Although the MPIH was developing well, I was mindful not to rush to launch it. Experiences both good and bad had taught me that plans such as these took a long time to come to fruition, especially when they were being created outside of official organisations and bodies.

To rush would mean that the product would not be properly researched and consulted on, leading to limited buy-in from those pivotal to its success, and the spectre of potential failure. I felt the resource was too vital to allow this to happen, so we took time to make sure all relevant parties were engaged and on board, to give it the best chance of success.

As I continued my work on developing and embedding the idea of MPIH into relevant organisations, Val published her own book about Damien's disappearance called *The Boy Who Disappeared*. Part memoir, part scathing review of the failures made by police in Damien's case, it brought home to me once again just how many families of the missing had been badly let down, and how much they were still suffering.

Little attention and next to no funding had been allocated to Damien's case for many years, with any action coming only from Val's dogged determination to demand support and investigation into potential new leads.

Her experience was markedly different to that of Kate and Gerry McCann. In the same year, 'Operation Grange' was granted a further £300,000 to continue up to March 2020, bringing the total investment in the UK's part of the search for Maddie to £11.75 million.[25]

There were always many reasons for the disparity in attention and funding for missing persons cases, of course, not least what type of news day it was when a person went missing.

Many factors came into play and there was no one definitive conclusion for why some cases gained more attention than others. Like everything in the world of the missing, it was complex and nuanced.

There was the 'mystery' element of Maddie's case – whether the circumstances of the disappearance managed to capture the imagination or fears of the public.

Val's campaign for 'Damien's Law' had highlighted the difference in response between missing girls and missing boys, and coverage of appeals for missing white women was also generally greater than those of other ethnicities. There were also suggestions that the type of image available in an appeal had an impact; an attractive woman or a cute, blonde little girl like Maddie would be more likely to generate more coverage than a tall, gangly teenage boy like Damien. But it wasn't just who the missing person was that determined interest and response. It was the type of people their families were too.

---

25 www.independent.co.uk/news/uk/home-news/madeleine-mccann-investigation-police-funding-home-office-year-a8945706.html

Kate and Gerry McCann were educated, confident and happy to put themselves out into the media glare. Similarly, despite the many years Damien's case had gone on, Val had somehow found the drive and determination to get out there and rally attention for his case, challenging authorities, banging on doors and speaking to media.

Some families did not have the confidence for public speaking and going out knocking on strangers' doors wasn't an easy thing to do. They might not trust the media, or the police for that matter, and so felt unable to engage.

Sometimes the emotional toll of having someone go missing meant that even individuals of a similar status and resources to the McCanns simply did not have the energy to keep the publicity machine going, or even put themselves in the spotlight in the first place. Others quite simply preferred to stay out of the public eye and grieve their loss in private.

But regardless of their personality types and how they responded to a loved one going missing, they *all* needed help. They all needed access to information and signposting to resources that could help them. They needed organisations that could address cases where the trail had gone cold and provide some hope for resolution.

They not only needed this help. They deserved it equally.

Dave's vision for a charity that would reinvestigate cold cases finally became a reality. After running a small pilot scheme since 2019 with police forces in Devon and Cornwall, Norfolk and Hampshire, Locate International was registered with the Charity Commission on 18 February 2022. I was proud to become the chair of the charity's Board of Trustees and continue to offer my expertise to help the organisation to this day.

Finally, after five years of hard work and development, we were finally able to begin to offer that to the world.

On Wednesday 25 May 2022, International Missing Children's Day, we finally launched the Missing Persons Information Hub. It had been a labour of love, and the product of our collective knowledge that better, more accessible information about missing persons was desperately needed.

It was an extremely proud moment, for me and the whole team who had been involved, but it was Val who best explained the importance of the information hub in a statement supporting the launch.

When your child is missing you are lost in time and space. The world continues its momentum, revolving around you whilst you are rooted to that spot in time. During my search for something, anything that might help me to understand, make sense of how I got here, I found a myriad of disembodied articles. I had an overwhelming need to understand the complexities of 'missing' and how to make it better for the next family who entered this dreadful situation. It took years to even realise I was searching for this clarity. I found information I wish I had known about when it first happened. Wondering how I had missed this or that which could have been helpful had someone mentioned it. But it was disjointed. It happened often enough to be very clear there was a disconnect. A central hub of information on missing issues was a vision that made so much sense to me.

As the website was launched, I thought about just how limited the tools at my disposal were when I had first been faced with Rob's case back in 1997. Over the years

I had equipped myself better, putting more tools in my metaphorical backpack, ready for when I needed them.

Now, after twenty-six years dedicated to work relating to missing persons, understanding the complexities and challenges, I was finally able to share those tools with anyone in the world who wished to access them.

Today, the police focus for missing persons is mainly on the here and now, the immediate cases and problems that are facing them. As they have limited resources, this is understandable. But is it correct?

What I will never understand is the decision made by the government to spend a huge sum of money on Operation Grange – £13.1 million between 2011 and June 2023[26] – when ownership of the case lay with the Portuguese police.

This is not to say that I don't believe Maddie's case warrants funds and attention. It deserves the best possible response, and everything should be done to find out what happened to her.

But why is it OK to give so much money to one case when others get little or no attention?

Was Kate and Gerry's pain any different from Val's?

Both lost a child. Both wanted the best possible response. Both still need answers and closure.

I still wonder how this spend could have been justified when, at the time, the NCA Missing Persons Unit reported over 11,000 unsolved missing person cases in the UK.

Shehzad Nawaz, Ellen Coss, Michael Bell, Carmel Fenech. Their names and those of their loved ones aren't likely to

26 www.independent.co.uk/news/uk/home-news/cost-of-madeleine-mccann-investigation-b2356431.html

be names that you've heard, like Maddie, Kate and Gerry, but their suffering and experiences are just as real.

Go to the 'Missing Appeals' page on Missing People's website and you can scroll through thousands of photos of individuals who are missing, many of them for years. To their families, they are just as important as Maddie.

Imagine what might have been possible had even a proportion of that £13.1 million been more equally distributed and used? How much more attention could have been given to those thousands of cases? What might it have meant to their families?

A lot of progress has been made since the early days when I first started this work and recognition has grown of just how important the subject of missing persons really is. Missing has also been recognised as being a key indicator of sexual exploitation and integral to many other forms of criminality and harm.

Yet it is still not perfect. We still see cases that are not dealt with as they should be, and in some cases missing people are not even reported as such because those around them do not recognise them as missing. There is still an enormous challenge to be tackled in defining exactly what missing is, so people – both the public and professionals – can recognise it in all its forms.

Missing is also something that can still draw extremely large amounts of publicity. But not *all* cases get publicity; some are reported briefly in newspapers or via the TV and radio, and a very small number get a significant amount.

This gives a distorted view of the situation to the public, not presenting the true scale of the issue. Observations from cases like those of Madeleine McCann and Damien Nettles provide some insight into the relevance of age, gender bias and the impact of the personalities, temperament and drive of the family of a missing person on media response.

But this is only part of the problem. In 2023, research from the charity Missing People, based on data from police forces and local authorities, revealed that people from minority ethnic groups went missing for longer, were less likely to be found by the police, and less likely to be recorded as being at risk than white people.[27] While we have come a long way, there are still so many disparities to be addressed.

Of all the lessons I have learned through my career, none have been more profound and often devastating than the human impact of a person going missing. According to data published by the National Crime Agency for the year 2020/21, there were 11,608 long-term missing person cases in England and Wales, Scotland and Northern Ireland. As a number alone, this is a shocking figure. But now consider it in terms of human impact.

That's 11,608 people who have gone missing due to difficult circumstances in their lives, or because they have potentially come to harm or been a victim of crime.

Then consider the people, like Val, who have been left behind. At a minimum that's potentially 11,608 people struggling with the practical and emotional difficulties that come with a missing loved one.

Research has also shown that an estimated 12 people are impacted by every missing person, so that human cost has the potential to be so much greater, growing to 139,296 people suffering, or even more.

---

27 www.missingpeople.org.uk/for-professionals/policy-and-research/information-and-research/research-about-missing/ethnicity-missing-people

Not many people really understand what the loss they experience is like, this 'ambiguous loss' that comes with no answers to questions about what happened to their missing loved one.

To try to illustrate this feeling and get people to better understand it, I often use a simple visualisation that we can all relate to.

I am sure that everyone who reads this book will have experienced the temporary loss of someone during their life. It may be that someone you know is unusually late home, not at the place where they were supposed to be or something similar.

Think about how you felt at that time. *Worried? Confused? Angry? Scared?*

For most of you this will have been short-lived, until the person turns up wondering what the fuss is about, or giving some rational explanation that sets your mind at ease.

Now, just imagine what it would be like if that person did not turn up at all. How would you feel as you were about to go to bed that night? Extend that to consider how you would feel a day, a week, a month, a year or even many years later.

That is what some people suffer, and I think it was beautifully illustrated by Val Nettles in March 2023 when she wrote about her son, Damien, who at the time had been missing for twenty-six years.

To Damien
   I don't know how to shake this feeling of perpetual anxiety. It's gnawing and tugging inwardly in my mind and in my soul.
   Never a day passes where I don't think of you

Damien.

*This feeling has sat with me daily since you went
missing. 26 years and counting my son without your
voice, your humour, and your smile and your very being.
The constant tug and pull aches of how much I miss you.
I think about you as I go about my daily routines. As if
I might seem normal, though it is grossly abnormal. Seen
by anyone who did not know my son vanished might
never suspect the pain inside my heart.*

*I wish you could have been with me longer. I know
something bad happened to take you from us dearest boy.
It's not your fault.*

*I just wish I knew. I wish I could find an answer to
make sense of all of this inner turmoil I suffer. But suffer
it all I will in hopes of knowing the truth one day.[28]*

People like Val and the thousands of other families of the
missing, who are still searching for answers, cannot and
should not be forgotten. It is important that we acknowledge their struggles and do what we can to provide help
and hope.

During 2022/23, Locate International's team of volunteer
investigators reviewed cases of 102 unidentified people and
22 missing persons. They resolved 70 cases. That's a resolution of one in two cases that they took on.

These resolved cases included a homeless man who was
found dead on the street in Chelsea, London in 1994. In
his possession was a diary with a name scrawled inside,
but at the time, the police had been unable to find his

---

28 www.valnettles.blogspot.com/2023/03/

family. When Locate investigated, almost twenty years later, they identified that the original investigation had interpreted the name in the diary incorrectly, misspelling it. With the correct spelling, Locate was able to find the identity of the man. Sadly, his parents had died without knowing what had happened to him, but friends were finally able to hold a memorial for him.

Another young man who had been found dead after being hit by a car had also been misidentified, but on reinvestigating the case, Locate was able to find his true identity and his family, let them know what had happened to him and support them in the aftermath of the news.

In 1994, a man rescued a father and son from the sea in England, but never returned to shore himself. He simply disappeared. Years later it was found that a body matching the description of the man had washed up on a beach in France, ten days after he had vanished. Organisations in the UK and France had been unable to exhume the body but Locate managed to facilitate this and is currently arranging a facial reconstruction in an attempt to finally confirm the man's identity.

If 12 people are affected by each missing person, then that means a potential 840 people received the answers they so desperately needed through Locate's work on these cases.

It is these families and friends of the missing, and those who go missing, that I most want my work to help. They should always have someone on their side: from the first day a person goes missing, until such a time when the case is resolved, or even when it is not. They should be seen, listened to and supported always.

CONCLUSION

I never had any great regard for what age I was. I didn't have a desire for big celebrations on 'milestone' birthdays, I certainly didn't let my age limit my activities and I didn't worry about getting older. To me my age was just a number – until I approached sixty-five in 2018.

Sixty-five was significant to me in a way that other landmark birthdays had not been. It represented something very specific – the age of retirement, the end of working life. I realised that for some it also implied the end of their useful life.

Business at the advisory was brisk, with a number of projects like my work with AMBER Alert Europe, training for ICMEC and consultancy work with Missing People still ongoing. I was busy, still travelling extensively, and my expertise was still frequently called upon, so I did not in any way feel redundant.

I was mindful of what I'd seen of my dad in retirement, often busier than he had been when he was working. He'd had his garden, an allotment, and was interested in church organs, so he apprenticed himself to a firm of organ builders to learn more. He was a church warden, loved woodwork and went to evening classes to learn wood carving, along with many other things that he filled his time with. Being busy and active kept him going, and he lived to the ripe age of ninety-three.

I realised that age manifested itself in different ways for different people. How many times had I looked at people and assessed how old I thought they were, only to get it very wrong? The thought also brought to mind my ex-colleagues who retired at a young age, as the police service allowed, and professed to doing very little. Some made it seem like they were living a dream, but I thought some of them looked old for their years.

Given that my life, working or otherwise, was showing no signs of slowing down, I was surprised how much the number drew my attention and made me think about what might be next for me.

As these thoughts circulated, a case that I had investigated in 2000, when I was around 47, resurfaced in my mind. A report had come in of a 65-year-old man, in good health, who had gone missing after attending the British Masters golf tournament.

The ticket had been purchased by the man's wife and was a gift celebrating his recent sixty-fifth birthday and retirement from work. According to her account, golf was something that he really enjoyed and being able to attend such a prestigious event was a real treat.

'He was excited to be going,' she said. 'I drove him to Woburn Golf Club, and we arranged for me to collect him afterwards. He said he would ring me when he was ready.'

The day passed and the tournament finished, but the call did not come. The man's wife became increasingly concerned for his safety. Of course, she tried to rationalise it in those first minutes. Maybe he had got a lift with someone else, or decided to go for a drink or something to eat before calling her?

'But that's just not like him,' she said. 'If plans changed, he'd call me.'

This information was vital for me. Acting completely out of character and doing things that they would not usually do was always a serious indicator of risk. I spoke to his wife in detail, trying to establish more about the circumstances of the day.

'Is there any reason you can think of for his disappearance?' I asked. 'Any problems that he was having? Was anything unusual that day?'

'Nothing at all,' she replied. 'We just made our way to the golf club. We stopped at a garage on the way so he could buy some sandwiches and a drink to take with him, and then I dropped him off.'

My ears pricked up. It was a seemingly innocuous comment, it might not mean anything, but details were important, and I knew immediately it was a line of enquiry that must be pursued. The wife explained how the man had emerged from the garage with his purchases in a carrier bag. She didn't see what he'd bought, and he'd taken the bag with him when he left her.

As I continued to interview the wife, extensive searches were being carried out at the golf course and in the woodland that surrounded it, in parallel with enquiries to find out if anyone had seen him on the day.

I also conducted further interviews with his friends and family, to see if I could develop a clearer picture of the man's life and his state of mind at the time. It emerged that the thought of reaching retirement age had hit him quite hard. He'd been depressed by the thought of stopping work and having no purpose in life.

Concerns were rising and I felt that familiar sense of dread in the pit of my stomach. Something felt amiss.

We needed to look further into the journey to the golf course for our answers. We found CCTV of him in the garage, selecting items. We couldn't make out what he purchased from the footage, due to the angle of the camera, but we noted that at one point he was not in the food and drink area of the shop.

What else was he buying? I thought.

I followed up with the garage staff, who were able to provide a copy of the till receipt, which itemised his purchases; some food, a drink . . .

A tow rope.

My concerns escalated immediately to the highest level. I knew there was no rational explanation for such a purchase that didn't suggest something more sinister. Putting all the information together and adding the context of the man's feelings about reaching retirement, I began to fear the worst.

That it was all too much, and he had planned to kill himself.

Sadly, a short while later, those fears were confirmed. During a search of the woodland surrounding the golf course, the man was found dead in what we subsequently learned was a favourite spot of his. There was no indication at all that anyone else had been involved. The death was recorded as suicide.

Although we'll never know for certain, it appears that the thought of retirement had been just too much for the man to deal with, seeming to think of it as the end of his useful life.

At the time, the case had been a reminder to me of the importance of understanding everything about the missing person, carrying out enquiries diligently and talking to the family on a regular basis, because not everything is revealed at the first time of asking. It was an example of putting all the pieces of the picture together, so we could understand what happened, and find him. In a professional sense, it was still a reminder of all those things – and the need to be thorough in all parts of the investigation, despite the outcome.

At the time I remember finding it extremely sad that a good man, who had led a good life, should find retirement so depressing. To me it only sounded like a good thing, free of the constraints of going to work and having freedom to do what I wanted.

Now as I was reaching the same age as that man, I could see his perspective a little more and it made me determined for it not to be a problem for me. Unlike other people approaching this milestone, I did have the advantage of having already retired twice – the first time from the police after thirty years' service, and the second time from the National Crime Agency. Each time I had managed OK.

Of course, this was largely by just continuing to work, but I imagined that my past 'retirements' were an indicator of how I was likely to behave in 'proper' retirement.

There was no strict rule that I *had* to stop. It was just when you *could* stop.

As far as I could see, I wasn't going to stop, either. My work wasn't just a job, it was something that mattered to me, and I planned to continue as long as I could – balanced with the possibility of having more time to do the things I wanted to do.

Thinking back to the man who took his life on reaching retirement, I considered how much of our self-worth and sometimes enjoyment is inextricably linked to our working life and professional success. Perhaps it was important to find that elsewhere as well, and the trick was to use your new-found free time to redirect your energies towards all those things you loved, or held an interest in, but didn't always have enough time to do?

I considered the many incredible hikes I'd enjoyed with friends, the holidays exploring countries around the globe with Shelley, my annual 'boys' adventure' holiday with Tom, spending a week away out in nature, cycling, walking or canoeing, and exploring new skills, like cooking, blacksmithing and off-road driving. These things all brought me a sense of enjoyment, achievement and purpose.

They were also so important to me that I made space for them while I was busy working. They would be there for me after I stopped, and I'd have even more time to give to them, with some space for new hobbies!

Albeit brief, I couldn't deny the passing discomfort that the idea of turning sixty-five caused me, but I was determined to ensure that my life would not lack value after I surpassed that magic number.

As it happened, the day came and went and I just carried on, as I had twice before.

As projects came to an end, I found that I wasn't keen to go chasing new contracts, but I still wanted to keep busy and do something that was helpful, so I decided to explore volunteer roles. Where did I want to spend this new time that I had available? What did I want to get out of it and what did I want to give back?

I knew I wanted to do something active, that would keep me fit and healthy, and I wanted to spend more time in my beloved outdoors, so when I saw that Evenley Wood Garden, not far from where I lived, was looking for volunteer gardeners, I decided to find out more.

Exploring the sixty acres of woodland that had been cultivated with trees and plants since the land's purchase in 1980, I was immediately taken by the garden. It was mature but continuously evolving, and although I was no expert plantsman, I was happy to get stuck in and work hard. I decided there and then to commit to two volunteer days a week.

It was physically demanding, being on the heavy end of gardening, working with trees and shrubs, not just bedding plants, but I loved the exertion, which was well balanced by the peaceful and restful nature of being out in the woods. Still working or seeing to family commitments three days a week, those two days became sacred and extremely therapeutic.

Sometimes, if a work or home issue occupied me, I'd question whether I should go to the gardens, or stay home to try and muddle through whatever challenge I was facing. But it would only be a fleeting consideration, and inevitably I would go. After a day of repairing wooden bridges, moving trees and shrubs, strimming, building and maintaining the paths and roads, I'd be tired but at peace.

Being in the wood alleviated my stress and left me refreshed and ready to manage whatever challenge it was I was facing. Some people paid good money for 'forest bathing'! I offered my time instead and reaped the same rewards.

One foot still in the working world, I also came across Medical Detection Dogs (MDD), an amazing charity that trains dogs to detect a variety of medical conditions, and support people with severe illnesses.

The charity had been established by Dr Claire Guest, whose pet Labrador, Daisy, took to nudging her breast so frequently that it made her think that something was amiss. Sure enough, a trip to her GP and subsequent tests resulted in the diagnosis of previously undetected cancer. Her experience prompted her to consider how to harness dogs' amazing sense of smell, and the charity was born.

One lady I met suffered from PoTS disease, a condition that resulted in her losing consciousness without warning. Her dog was trained to detect such episodes, alert her, and enable her to get into a safe place where she would not fall over, or hurt herself.

'It's changed my life,' she told me. 'I can live in a more normal way and without fear now.'

Having worked with dogs during my police career and being an animal lover, I was fascinated and wanted to be involved, so I volunteered as a driver, gardener and general handyman and was having a wonderful time. Retirement wasn't panning out to be all that bad at all. In fact, I was quite enjoying it. But then, in March 2020, everything changed.

Throughout my career, I have witnessed how anyone could suddenly find themselves affected by someone going missing. It is not something that happens exclusively to individuals of a certain age, gender or background. No one is immune from it happening to them.

In most cases, those left behind simply never see it coming, and why would they?

I remember once meeting a woman with a stable family life and a good career high up in social services. She was accustomed to dealing with the challenges faced by children in the care system and the issue of going missing. You would think she would be the last person to be personally affected by it. Yet her daughter had gone missing because she was being sexually exploited and the perpetrators had taken control of her life.

In life generally, as in the missing, there are things that none of us see coming, like the Covid-19 pandemic. Who could have imagined a nationwide order to stay indoors, save for an hour's worth of government-mandated exercise per day, no further than five miles from your own front door?

We – Shelley, the boys and I, like many others – just got on with it and accepted there was little we could do to change things. It was tough, but others were suffering far worse. We were lucky, or so we thought.

Then Matt, Shelley's eldest, caught Covid. It was unpleasant, but not a problem in itself, until Matt had his vaccination booster, after waiting the requisite time after infection. Very shortly after, he felt unwell. A fit and healthy young man in his twenties who had not seen the doctor since he was five, he ended up in hospital for a week, seriously ill and suffering from a reaction to the booster that had triggered type 1 diabetes, Addison's disease and hypothyroidism.

The combination of these three diseases mean that Matt now has life-changing conditions that require a complex regime of medication and careful management – and manage it Matt does, informed by lots of careful research and without any drama. As he puts it: 'It is what it is.'

There are always things that happen in life that will blindside us, that will change everything and set our lives on completely unexpected courses. We cannot control whether these things happen or not, but we have the power to choose how we respond. That is what determines what happens in the aftermath.

The pandemic also saw my business change over-night, as travel became impossible and meetings, calls and conferences were hastily adapted to be conducted online. With a reduction in the amount of work to be done, and some of my usual leisure-time activities on hold, I had more time to sit and reflect on my life and work.

One obvious observation was just how much time I'd spent travelling to meetings that it was now becoming apparent could just as easily have been done online, from home. I also noted that I had actually been quite happy that my work was reducing and thought it would allow me to move into retirement proper.

But, even in the depths of a global pandemic, it seemed I still had difficulty saying 'No'. When MDD launched a research project to find out if dogs could be used to detect Covid, Claire came to me to help with mapping some of their processes, using my expertise in doing similar with processes around missing persons and other policing issues.

This task was not as a volunteer but as a paid consultant. Work somehow always found me.

It was a fascinating project, so of course I agreed. I also decided to take on a fostering role for one of their dogs. I initially took on a big black Labrador, Reggie, to work on his attachment issues, and then Meg, another young Labrador, became part of our family.

My thought that life would taper naturally into retirement had turned out to be a false assumption.

The plan since 'retiring' for the third time has always been to keep busy. Sometimes it gets a bit too busy, but most of the time I honestly wouldn't have it any other way. It is just how I am.

I do wonder if I would be this way had I not found those papers relating to a missing person case gone wrong on my desk nearly twenty-seven years ago. There is no doubt that Rob's case changed my life, and I am grateful for the purpose that being assigned to it gave me. I saw in his family the pain that was caused by a loved one going missing, and how that could be exacerbated by ineptitude and a lack of sensitivity. From that moment on, I never wanted to see another family have an experience like that.

While I have done my best to spearhead change, I still have seen it many times since. My mission is far from complete.

As might be expected, the Covid-19-impacted year of 2020/21 had a significant effect on missing behaviour. The NCA's 2020/21 Missing Persons Data Report highlighted a decrease in the number of individuals reported as missing across almost all forces, with the number of missing reports dropping to 241,000 from the previous year's 359,000 (2019/20).

In 2020/21, there were 17.8 per cent fewer missing-related calls in England and Wales compared with forces supplying data the previous year. Scotland experienced a 48.3 per cent reduction and PSNI experienced a 21.3 per cent reduction.

In 2021/22, the number of missing reports returned to pre-pandemic levels, with police receiving 330,000 reports of missing people during that year. With the exception of that Covid-19-impacted year, the volume of missing-related incidents has been fairly consistent since 2016.

People may assume that if numbers are not going up, that's a good thing. But my question is, why are they not coming down? If we accept that missing is an indicator for some form of harm or crisis, should we really be pleased that the same steady number of people are reaching that point each year?

While some statistics around the missing can, on the surface, appear reassuring, such as most missing adults return within 48 hours, and less than 1 per cent of cases remain unresolved after 28 days. But I ask you to consider everything I have shared in this book and ask yourself, are those statistics really as comforting as they seem?

Yes, these people came back. But what happened to them when they were away? What harm did they come to and what impact will this have on their lives?

If someone feels the need to go missing, there must be something happening in their life that drives them to it. It is quite clear in my mind that everyone who goes missing suffers some form of harm, and research clearly supports our belief that the official data is a gross underestimate of the true picture.

The latest NCA Missing Persons Unit annual report for 2021/22 halves the previous figure for outstanding unsolved cases, which may look like positive progress. That is until you learn that the Met, the UK's largest police force, did not provide any data. If it had, based on the previous year's data, it is likely that number would have been in excess of 12,000 – so an increase instead of a decrease.

To this day, there are significant flaws in the reporting and recording practices around missing persons. Different data is recorded by different forces in different ways. A national recording system has been discussed for many years, starting around the time of 'Missing You Already', but never implemented. Different processes are used, and supported by the *Still Running* research series, I strongly believe this means that both figures for the missing and harm suffered is going vastly under-reported. What frustrates me most deeply is that this was a lesson I learned when I started my PRAS research project, not long after dealing with Rob's and the gentleman with dementia's cases.

If I learned these lessons in 2000, why is there so much that has not moved on in the last twenty-four years? The risk matrix that we use is still based on professional opinion and not the research I have advocated for over this time.

I do believe that the various guidance, frameworks and tools that I have been responsible for developing have helped to make a difference. In every case I have been involved in I have always tried my very best to get the job done quickly, professionally and with sensitivity. I have made a career of addressing things that I believe have not been done properly and tried to improve them.

But that is not to say I have always done the right thing. I may be a missing persons expert, but I too have made wrong choices, lost vital time and missed things. It is in these moments that I have learned some of my most important lessons.

I was once managing a search for a missing man where an area of woodland was our focus. The search teams came back, reported that their areas were clear, and so we moved on. But a couple of days later, the family of the missing man found him dead in that very same wood.

It was a dreadful discovery for them, and I could not understand how he could have been missed. I went back to the search team, and they told me that they had been unable to enter that particular area as they were confronted by a gamekeeper carrying a shotgun who told them to get off the land, which they understandably did. But, too afraid to admit they had not done their job properly, they had not let me know. Had I known, the outcome would not have been different, but the family would have been spared that terrible discovery.

As humans we find it difficult to admit when we have made a mistake, or not completed a set task very well, but this is just one example of why it is so important to be honest about these things, and why we should always own up to our mistakes.

When I look back on my career, there are missing person cases that I know I could and should have dealt with better, even though they were a product of their time and the processes that existed when I first set out on this journey. Back then, nobody had really thought about what we were doing right or wrong and nothing was being done to change it. I cannot correct the mistakes I may have made in those earlier years, but I have always sought to recognise and own them and make improvements for the future.

I have also made mistakes during the latter part of my career. Recently, I undertook a live interview discussing the case of Nicola Bulley, who at the time was still missing from Lancashire. Her body had not yet been found and there was massive speculation around the case. The press and social media coverage was at an unprecedented level, and I recognised how hard this must have been for the friends and family, especially when there were wild accusations being made about anyone and anything.

I took part in a number of media interviews, trying to be the voice of reason against all of the speculation that was out there. It was in the live broadcast that I made a dreadful mistake. I had known where I wanted to go with the conversation and was doing my best to stick to my line, as many years of media training had taught me. But the interviewer was posing new questions to me, bringing up other information that started to fill my brain.

I had referenced Damien Nettles' unsolved case, intending to say that Damien had disappeared and had never been found. But with Nicola having gone missing near a river, the talk of water was so prevalent and a hotly debated hypothesis. As I spoke about Damien, unintentionally I said that he had 'gone into the water when he disappeared'. At the time, I didn't even realise I'd said it. It was only when I received an understandably upset and angry email from Val's daughter, Sarah, that it clicked.

I was mortified because I understood what this would mean to the family. Not only was there absolutely no evidence to support that theory, so it was completely wrong for me to say, but it was also a hypothesis that the family had spent years batting off. They knew that if Damien's disappearance was confined to a box – in this case the 'gone in the water' box – it would stay in that very box.

While they are realistic as a family, given the passage of time, they are extremely aware that they still need to keep that box open so all possibilities can continue to be explored. My words were damaging to that. I am sure they felt let down by someone they thought of as a trusted friend, and I was horrified by the hurt I knew that I had caused.

I apologised personally and publicly to Val and the family, made a statement correcting what I'd said and jumped on any conversations on social media to clarify what I had meant to say. Val responded in her typical gracious manner, and accepted my apology, but I'd like to take the opportunity to say sorry once again for this mistake.

We cannot be perfect, but we can take ownership for our mistakes, and seek to do better in future.

There is no doubt that we have come a long way since I started on this journey and so many things are better. The old-school attitude of 'just another misper' thankfully has almost disappeared. Most, if not all, UK police forces have dedicated individuals or units in place to manage missing persons which is so valuable and keeps a focus on the issue. There is better recognition of vulnerabilities and higher risk cases, with 2021/22 data showing that 14,568 incidents were reported with a CSE flag and 39,180 incidents with a mental health flag. Yet despite this progress there are still gaps, as data reporting is not complete across all forces.

How can we ever get the true picture? Why do we not have that national reporting system that has been discussed for so many years?

Yes, we have better processes and procedures for dealing with missing persons cases, alert systems, trained family liaison officers to support families and ways of working internationally. But despite all this, sometimes I see the same mistakes I witnessed more than two decades ago playing out again in exactly the same way, and I wonder if we have learned anything at all.

I was recently referred to a distraught father whose son had gone missing some months earlier. As he explained how the case had been dealt with, my heart sank. The procedures were not much different from those that existed at the start of my journey: lack of empathy, poor communication, limited updates and very little in the way of support for the family. There was no understanding of the parents' needs, poorly worded communications that sought to justify lack of action and promises that were not kept.

Time had dragged on until one day, the father received a telephone call from a police officer.

'Some remains have been found; we think they might be your son,' the officer said.

Although horrified and devastated, the father had thought that finally they would know what had happened to their boy, and they could allow themselves to grieve. They prepared themselves for further updates.

But none came. In fact, for nearly two weeks there was complete radio silence, so the parents were once again at a loss.

We still have a long way to go. I think that this is perhaps why I carry on. Right now, I am working with Safe and Found Online, helping to develop the way protocols for potential missing persons are stored and made available to the police when needed, with a plan to put them securely online.

These mainly relate to existing protocols for people living with dementia (Herbert Protocol, 2011), children in care (Philomena Protocol, 2019), and those with mental health issues (Ellam Protocol, 2021). I have also worked with others to develop and launch a new protocol for ex-military veterans vulnerable to going missing and suicidal ideation (Forcer Protocol, 2023), which began a six-month trial with Greater Manchester Police on Armistice Day in 2023. In my experience, it was met with unprecedented support from government ministers, police, veterans, their families and NGOs.

When someone goes missing, the person reporting can often be upset and panicked, making it harder to recall important information when it is most needed. I have dealt with too many cases where people from these more vulnerable groups have gone missing, and we have not had all the relevant information when we needed it. As a result, they have ended up in places where they could have been found and not lost their lives if we had more information upon which to base our search and investigation strategies.

If these risk factors are known, and the fact that these individuals are more vulnerable to going missing is known and acknowledged, it allows those close to or responsible for them to prepare accordingly. If the protocol forms are readily available online, everything can be written down in advance, in a calm atmosphere, improving the chances of recording the essential information accurately. Should they go missing, critical information can instantly be available to the police, enabling the best possible response.

If you have someone who is at risk of going missing through these types of situations, trust me when I tell you that taking the time to fill out and submit a protocol form could save their life. But I also understand that it is not easy.

In recent years, my sister Sue's partner, Bill, has been diagnosed with Alzheimer's disease. We watch as his condition deteriorates, and he ceases to be the person he was, as though a curtain is being drawn and he is gradually disappearing. It is heartbreaking and devastating for my dear sister. A true countryman, throughout his life Bill loved nothing better than to walk outdoors, something that had not left him. This led me to see the immediate need to complete a Herbert Protocol form due to his increased risk of walking away from home, but something stopped me. I was having to admit his frailty and even I found it hard to take the step that would somehow confirm that. It had to be overcome and the form was completed. But it made me realise that if I found it difficult, with all of my knowledge and experience, how difficult could it be for other people? Another lesson learned.

When a new challenge inevitably seeks me out, I have always immediately said: 'Yes, I can do that.' Even today, I do it all the time. Sometimes, though, as the words escape my mouth, I'll wonder why on earth I've agreed and why I just can't keep quiet.

Although my two days at Evenley still remain sacred for my gardening, the rest of the time Meg sits curled up at my feet, wondering why my laptop is getting more attention than her, and why we're not heading off to the woods where she accompanies me on my volunteering duties. I think about everything that I have outside of work: loving family and friends, a wonderful relationship with my son, Tom, a life of laughter and adventure with Shelley, and her two boys, both of whom continue to thrive and succeed despite the challenges they face, and of course, Meg. Her big eyes beg 'Can we go out?' and I'm almost convinced.

But I realise that my ability to keep saying 'Yes' to my work is a privilege. I know that not everyone is so lucky. This world that I have inhabited for so long – the complex, fascinating and all-consuming world of the missing – is what has made me the person I am today. It has drawn out skills and abilities that I did not realise I possessed and led to experiences that I could never have imagined. But it has also taught me lessons about myself that have shaped how I look after myself, the choices I have made and the relationships I have built.

There have been moments when the fragility of life has really been brought home to me. One time Tom was stung by a wasp while out walking with me and Shelley. Face swollen beyond recognition, we rushed him to the nearest hospital, which was still working under Covid restrictions. Terrified, we had to send him through the door and wait outside for news. He'd had a severe allergic reaction and returned with an EpiPen that is now never out of his possession.

Another time I found myself at home in pain and without any memory of what had happened to me. The last thing I could remember was that I had been out on a bike ride, and everything else was a blank. After extensive tests, I was told that I had suffered transient global amnesia (TGA), a rare condition mainly occurring in those over fifty while exercising. TGA is a sudden, temporary interruption of short-term memory. I learned that, when experiencing one, you can be disoriented, not know where you are or be confused about time, but otherwise be alert, attentive and have normal thinking abilities. The only other evidence of what might have happened was my cycle helmet, which was split down the middle. Whatever did happen, I know I was very lucky and realise the outcome could have been very different. Thankfully, I have been told there is no known reason for TGA happening and that it rarely recurs.

It is reasons like this – among so many others – that I do not take for granted that I am still physically and mentally able to do what I do. I am also extremely grateful that I still have the passion and determination for my work in the missing. I am not extraordinary, but I have been on an extraordinary journey, and I am absolute proof that anything is possible if you have that passion and determination to do it.

I might have reached an age where I should be retiring, but will my work with the missing ever let me? I'm not sure it will, and I'm not sure I want it to. As long as I am able, and as long as I have the drive and desire to do so, I will continue to try to make things better for the missing and the people they leave behind. I will be the one that won't keep quiet, who will step up to the challenge and will do whatever I can to change things for the better.

'Sort this out, will you, Charlie?'

Yes, of course I will.

AFTERWORD

While I was working on 'Missing You Already', I met John Bennett. John had been a detective superintendent and the senior investigating officer for the Cromwell Street murders in Gloucester, committed by Fred and Rosemary West. It's a case that needs little introduction due to the infamy of the couple and the shocking and prolific nature of their crimes. Rosemary West was jailed in 1995 for the murder of ten young girls and women. Her husband, Fred, killed himself before standing trial. They had preyed on vulnerable young girls and women, playing out depraved sexual fantasies, which eventually led to murder.

As we talked about the case and the lessons that he had learned from it, he shared how it had driven him to work more generally in the field of missing persons. He retired from the force and worked for the charity Missing People (formerly the National Missing Persons Helpline). We had similar thoughts and aims in relation to the missing. Like other people I have met who had worked on major cases, the experience had significantly impacted him. When I met with him at his home, his wife was clearly supportive, but could not bear to be in the same room as us as he trawled through his memories once again. He often appeared haunted by the case and unable to let go.

For those working in missing persons, looking back can be an upsetting experience. But we can often only move forward by looking back and learning from the past, which I believe is essential and that is what I am doing with this book. One of the reasons I was persuaded to write it is the hope that it will be a further prompt for action and change. I continue to be involved in missing because I see there is still much to be done.

I think of myself as ordinary, not exceptional. From a nice but normal background, and lucky to find myself where I am today. So, when I was sent an email asking me to write a book about my life working in missing persons, I was nothing short of amazed. Shortly before this invitation – which I believed to be spam until I received a follow-up phone call – I had been sitting at home with my wife, Shelley, discussing the many unexpected trajectories of my career. She asked me what I would do with the accumulated knowledge and experience from my work, the various publications, websites and other records.

My immediate and flippant response was 'Put it in the bin'. However, on reflection I have recognised that many of the experiences I have had *are* worth sharing. For many years now it has been my mission to help people understand what 'missing' really means. Telling my own story is another way to do that.

Shelley's question also prompted me to consider what had driven me throughout my career and how I arrived here. In many cases I've been carried along by circumstance; being involved in cases that brought me to the attention of others, being asked to contribute based on my past experiences, being in the right (and sometimes wrong) place at the right time. But not all of this can be circumstance. At any point I could have said no, taken a different route, but I didn't.

One day in 2000, my friend Simon and I undertook the West Coast Trail on Vancouver Island, a 46-mile trek that takes 6 to 8 days to walk due to the extremely difficult terrain. There were no facilities on the route and everything you needed to survive had to be carried in your rucksack. As we planned our hike, we learned the route was originally created as a rescue path for the survivors of shipwrecks who, until it existed, would go missing and die. I was fascinated by the idea that someone, somewhere had decided to tread a path that had not before been trodden to create a safe route of passage, creating a lifeline for those who found themselves in peril. I wondered how they did it, what tools they used and why they, unlike others, survived.

It took some time before I saw synergy between that hike and my own journey in the missing. The journey has seen tremendous highs and lows, but each challenge met and faced has ensured a clearer, safer route to traverse when working with the missing.

ACKNOWLEDGEMENTS

Along my journey many people have played an important part in my life and there are some that I would like to mention and apologise to many others I have omitted.

Shelley and the boys, for their support and tolerance as I pursued my obsession with missing persons, growing to accept seeing my suitcase packed and ready for yet another trip away.

Those senior officers in the police who supported me, believed in me and said the right things at critical points along my journey, especially Paul West, John Reeve, Peter Hilton, Mick Page and Peter Neyroud.

My long-distance walking buddies, Simon and Mark – who was also a great listener in times of trouble.

Joe Apps, my manager at the Missing Persons Bureau for trusting me and letting me do it my way.

Val Nettles for broadening my understanding of what it was like to be the mother of a son who had disappeared and opening my mind to those wider issues.

Nikki Croft-Girvan for helping me make sense of my ramblings and making them readable. Beth Eynon and the team at Orion Books for finding me and making this a reality.

My parents. Having me later in life they endured the early days when they were not always rewarded by seeing me succeed. It saddens me that they died before the good things happened and I wish they had seen what I have achieved.

FURTHER READING

Publications authored by Charlie Hedges:
Missing You Already
ACPO Guidance on Missing 2005
ACPO Practice Advice on Search 2006
A Code of Practice for The Police Service on Collecting
    and Sharing Data on Missing Persons with Public
    Authorities 2008
ACPO Guidance on Missing 2010
ACPO Interim Guidance on Missing 2013
Understanding and Managing Risk in the Context of
    Missing Persons 2016
Understanding and Managing Risk in the Context of
    Missing Persons 2020
MPIH Families Guidance 2022

Publications with Charlie Hedges as co-author or contributor:
Statutory Guidance on Children Who Run Away or Go
    Missing from Home or Care 2013
Moving On from Munro: Improving Children's Services
    2014
Rapid Emergency Child Alert System Framework
    ICMEC 2016
ICMEC Photo Distribution Framework 2017
Missing Persons: A Handbook of Research

There is no comprehensive list of missing persons that is available to the public. Some information is made available through the below sources:

The UK Missing Persons Unit lists unidentified persons on their website:
www.missingpersons.police.uk/en-gb/case-search

Missing People has a searchable list of records they hold:
www.missingpeople.org.uk/appeal-search

Locate International display the cases they are reviewing on their website:
www.locate.international